This Diary
Will Change
Your Life
2007

# Instructions

Welcome! By purchasing *This Diary Will Change Your Life* or accepting it as a gift, you commit yourself to following the weekly tasks contained herein to the letter, and to report your progress back to authors Benrik via www.thiswebsitewillchangeyourlife.com. The Diary's "extreme self-improvement" philosophy is based on permanent revolution in people's lives and imaginations. Thus it is imperative to actually follow its tasks for real, regardless of petty practical, legal or moral considerations. Otherwise, quantifiable life-change is not guaranteed.

Good luck, and enjoy the year 2007!

## Benrik Limited

Benrik are Ben Carey and Henrik Delehag. They are mainly known for *This Diary Will Change Your Life*, now in its fourth year with over 350,000 copies sold worldwide, leaving a mere 6,499,650,000 still to go. They believe that contemporary life is due for a thorough shake-up, and have channelled that belief into publishing, rather than into a time-consuming global jihad. They have accumulated tens of thousands of devotees around the world, and are prepared to rent them out for suitable occasions, including birthdays, bar mitzvahs and counter-insurgency work. To join them, visit www.thiswebsitewillchangeyourlife.com, where you may start your own blog and undergo your life-change in public. Please note: Benrik have now registered as a religion, so any unwarranted criticism may be liable under the Religious Hatred Act 2006.

Please refer to the back of the Diary, where you will find official portraits of Benrik to hang above your bed and inspire you in your "extreme self-improvement" efforts.

## Personal details

Name:............................................................................................................

Surname:........................................................................................................

Date of birth:................................................................................................

Address:..........................................................................................................

Country:..........................................................................................................

Home phone number:....................................................................................

Office phone number:..................................................................................

Mobile phone number:................................................................................

E-mail:............................................................................................................

Role model:....................................................................................................

Aspiration in life:........................................................................................

Childhood dream:........................................................................................

Definition of beauty:..................................................................................

Explanation of evil:....................................................................................

## Collective tasks

This seal indicates a collective task.
These tasks harness the power of
thousands of Diary readers, acting in
unison around the world to produce
life-changing results on a global scale

## Mood chart

Orgasmic
Over the moon
Happy as Larry
Fine, thank you!
OK
So-so
Pissed off
Mad as hell
Deeply depressed
Suicidal

It is crucial to monitor your mental state as you follow the Diary's prescriptions.
Fill in the weekly mood charts by plotting your mood level every day of the week,
and if your mood dips below the dotted line, seek immediate help. Compare your
mood to the World Mood...

# 2007 SCHEDULE

**Week 1** Induction Week: Let Benrik stamp your passport ■

**Week 2** Knock on every door you see ■

**Week 3** Spy on your parents ■

**Week 4** Paris Hilton Week ■

**Week 5** Join extremist organizations and out-extreme them ■

**Week 6** Leave your wallet on the street ■

**Week 7** Pick a partner based on genetic superiority ■

**Week 8** Draft your speech to the UN ■

**Week 9** Tell everyone you've just won the lottery ■

**Week 10** Only do things you have never done before ■

**Week 11** "Glorify" terrorism ■

**Week 12** Bribe people ■

**Week 13** Kill a commercial ■

**Week 14** Enter Miss or Mr World ■

**Week 15** Claim to see the Virgin Mary in an everyday object ■

**Week 16** Have a nervous breakdown ■

**Week 17** Help finish roadworks ■

**Week 18** Golden Bookmark Week ■

**Week 19** Demonstrate in favour of the government ■

**Week 20** Smile inappropriately ■

**Week 21** Positive Discrimination Week ■

**Week 22** Groom someone on the net ■

**Week 23** Disgrace Week ■

**Week 24** Follow your body clock ■

**Week 25** Swap blood with another Benrik reader ■

**Week 26** Gatecrash the news ■

**Week 27** Answer spam emails ☐

**Week 28** Wear a burka ☐

**Week 29** Sleep in public ☐

**Week 30** Check that your sex life is normal ☐

**Week 31** Everyone invade the Danish village of Svankær ☐

**Week 32** Opt out of the internet ☐

**Week 33** Do something that passers-by will never forget ☐

**Week 34** Advise your military ☐

**Week 35** Subliminal Week ☐

**Week 36** Switch on your appendix ☐

**Week 37** Parasite Week: Live at the expense of others ☐

**Week 38** See a dead body ☐

**Week 39** Start a business empire from your garage ☐

**Week 40** Monopolize radio phone-ins ☐

**Week 41** Let the skeletons out of your closet ☐

**Week 42** Go on hunger strike ☐

**Week 43** Dig a tunnel to the other side of the world ☐

**Week 44** Send your DNA to the authorities ☐

**Week 45** Become spokesperson for your neighbourhood ☐

**Week 46** Hug every tree you walk past ☐

**Week 47** Erect a statue of yourself in a public place ☐

**Week 48** Increase your pain threshold ☐

**Week 49** Befriend a customer-care person ☐

**Week 50** Walk into a police station and give yourself up ☐

**Week 51** Adopt a Christmas turkey ☐

**Week 52** Doomsday Week: Prepare for the impending apocalypse ☐

# LET BENRIK STAMP YOUR PASSPORT

Welcome to 2007, and congratulations on your new Diary! To induct you symbolically into the Benrik community, we require that you send us your passport this week, so that we may stamp it with the Benrik logo. This will confirm your commitment to the life-changing programme, and make you truly "one of us". From hereon in, there is no turning back...

Dear Benrik,

Please stamp my passport (enclosed) as proof of my membership. I have read the terms and conditions opposite and agree to them.

Name:.........................................................................

Date:...........................................................................

Signature:...................................................................

Attach this application form to your passport

| Monday 1 | New Year's Day | Tuesday 2 | Bank Holiday (Scotland) | Wednesday 3 |
|---|---|---|---|---|

Thursday 4

MOOD CHART

8

7

6

5

4

3

2

1

MON   TUE   WED   THU   FRI   SAT   SUN

| Friday 5 | Saturday 6 | Sunday 7 |
|---|---|---|

Induction Week: Let Benrik stamp your passport

**Monday 8**

**Tuesday 9**

**Wednesday 10**

**Thursday 11**

**Friday 12**

**Saturday 13**

**Sunday 14**

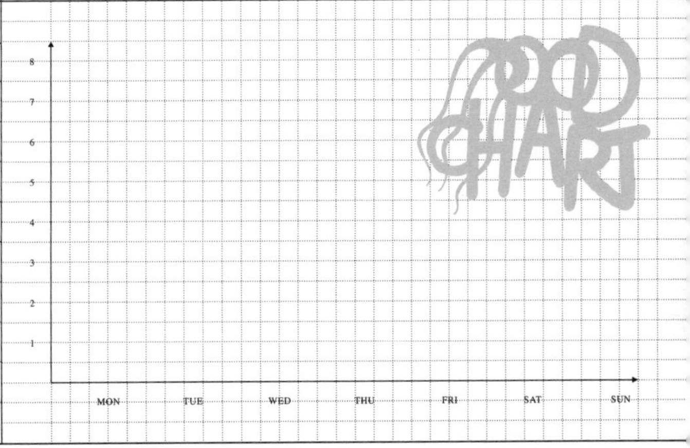

POP CHART

8

7

6

5

4

3

2

1

MON   TUE   WED   THU   FRI   SAT   SUN

Knock on every door you see

# This week knock on every door you see

Crack den

Albanian Mafiosi holding a
businessman hostage

Wife in bed with a man
not her husband

Sudanese refugee who
used to be a king

Our daily routines take us past hundreds of doors, most of which have effectively become invisible to us, but each of which conceals a whole new world waiting to be discovered. This week, knock on those doors and find out what lies behind them. Show the Diary if it helps, but obey this one rule: if you are lucky enough to be invited in, you must accept. Down the rabbit-hole you go…

*Here are some typical closed doors with what lies behind them:*

Broom cupboard

Gateway to parallel universe

Children who have tied up their babysitter and are watching forbidden TV programmes

Most beautiful woman in the world crying with loneliness

# This week, spy on your parents

Your mother and father are key figures in your life, but what do you actually know about them? What are they really like when you're not around? Are they indeed who they say they are? How do you even know for sure they are your real parents? Follow them in the street. Listen in on their phone calls. Interrogate them and others who may know the truth. Investigate them fully this week and confront them with the results.

### 1. INTERROGATE: MOTHER
Some memories don't lie. Even if it's slightly embarrassing, ask your mother if you may breastfeed again for a minute, and check that the experience matches your recollections.
RESULTS:
Breasts feel familiar.............................+2pts
Breasts feel foreign..............................-2pts
Breasts feel arousing............................-7pts

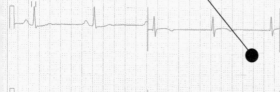

### 4. INTERROGATE: ELDERLY RELATIVE
Every self-respecting family features a senile relative who has forgotten everything except for the darkest family secrets. Get them drunk on gin and find out if anything was kept from you.
RESULTS:
You were found..................................-7pts
You were adopted................................-8pts
You were sent from planet Krypton..........-9pts

### 5. INTERROGATE: NEIGHBOURS
Neighbours have a front-row seat in the drama of your family life. And unlike relatives, they are an unbiased source of gossip. If there's the slightest peccadillo in your parents's past, they'll know it.
RESULTS:
Your mother is cheating on your father..........................-5pts
Your father is cheating on your mother..........................-5pts
Both of them are wife-swapping with the neighbours...-3pts

## 2. INTERROGATE: FATHER

These days, paternity can be established very
easily, with a simple genetic test. If your father is
the real thing, he will not mind donating a hair,
a nail or a small blood sample for this purpose.
RESULTS:
DNA matches yours exactly.........................+2pts
DNA does not match yours exactly...............-1pt
DNA is not human........................................-5pts

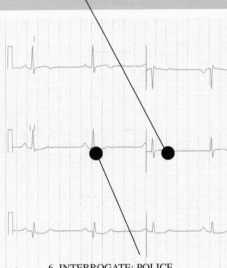

## 3. INTERROGATE: DOCTOR

Track down the doctor whose name appears on
your birth certificate and show him a photo of
your parents. Can he or she confirm your so-called
mother and father were both present at your birth?
RESULTS:
Both present...................................................+4pts
One present.....................................................+1pt
Neither present...............................................-3pts

## 6. INTERROGATE: POLICE

If people have anything serious to hide, it's probably
tucked away in their police record. Visit your local
police station and share your suspicions. Ask if you can
comb through your parents's files in search of clues.
RESULTS:
Records are clean.....................................+2pts
Records have been tampered with........................-2pts
Records show you were kidnapped as a child but
the ransom was never paid and so your "parents"
have kept you ever since....................................-15pts

Recommendations
More than 0 points: Your family is far too normal. Keep looking for clues.
0 to -20 points: Your parents are more of a mess than you thought, and
have probably passed it on to you.
Over -20 points: You have grounds for divorce from your parents.
Speak to a family lawyer immediately.

# January 15–21

**Monday 15**

...........................................................................
...........................................................................
...........................................................................
...........................................................................
...........................................................................
...........................................................................
...........................................................................
...........................................................................

**Tuesday 16**

**Wednesday 17**

**Thursday 18**

...........................................................................
...........................................................................
...........................................................................
...........................................................................
...........................................................................
...........................................................................
...........................................................................
...........................................................................
...........................................................................

MOOD CHART

8
7
6
5
4
3
2
1

MON   TUE   WED   THU   FRI   SAT   SUN

**Friday 19**

**Saturday 20**

**Sunday 21**

Spy on your parents

## Monday 22

## Tuesday 23

## Wednesday 24

## Thursday 25

## Friday 26

## Saturday 27

## Sunday 28

CHART

| | MON | TUE | WED | THU | FRI | SAT | SUN |

8
7
6
5
4
3
2
1

Paris Hilton Week

# Paris Hilton Week

Benrik recommend Paypal!

This week, upload a clip of yourself having sex onto the internet. In a world of spin, watching someone you know having intercourse is paradoxically one of the few authentic experiences still available, which is why it has such appeal. And best of all, there is no stigma attached to it these days (as long as your partner is a fully-consenting adult).

Making £££££ from it: Unless you're an heiress, a celebrity, extremely good-looking, or preferably all of the above, you will have trouble attracting a wider audience. Instead, focus on your core target market: people who already know you. If you include friends, distant relatives and colleagues, you probably know upwards of 200 people who would pay hard cash to see you in action. At £5 each, that makes a cool £1,000. Not bad for an evening's work.

# This week, join extremist organizations and out-extreme them

**BNP**

Organization: **BRITISH NATIONAL PARTY**
Extreme beliefs: Calls for an immediate halt to all further immigration, the immediate deportation of criminal and illegal immigrants, and the resettlement of immigrants who are legally here. Also calls for restoration of capital punishment.
How to join them: Membership is open to those of British or kindred European ethnic descent. Join at enquiries@bnp.org.uk.
How to out-extreme them: "Foreign tourists come over here and sleep with our women. Ban tourism pronto!"

**AF**

Organization: **ANARCHIST FEDERATION**
Extreme beliefs: The Anarchist Federation is an organization of class-struggle anarchists which aims to abolish capitalism, all hierarchy and all oppression to create a free worldwide classless equal society: anarchist communism.
How to join them: Email your membershp enquiry with name and postal address to: join@afed.org.uk.
How to out-extreme them: "Any organization is intrinsically hierarchical and fascist. Let's disband immediately!"

**ALF**

Organization: **ANIMAL LIBERATION FRONT**
Extreme beliefs: Animals are our brothers and sisters in other species. They have equal rights and therefore need protecting by direct action against all forms of animal abuse, including in particular animal testing.
How to join them: Try contacting them via the Animal Liberation Press Office, BM4400, London, WC1N 3XX.
How to out-extreme them: "Don't insects have equal rights too? Kill the fly killers!"

There is something appealingly old-fashioned about people who hold extreme views, something medieval about their blind certainties and the lengths to which they will go to advance their cause. This week, join some of these organizations, learn from their resolve, and test their grip on rational thought by suggesting even more extreme views and seeing if they embrace them.

**ELF**

Organization: **EARTH LIBERATION FRONT**
Extreme beliefs: The environment must be protected by "ecotage" (ecological sabotage), which involves inflicting economic damage on those who profit from the destruction and exploitation of the Earth.
How to join them: The E.L.F. has no centralized organization to contact. You could always try to attend an Earth First Gathering (efgathering@aktivix.org) and hope that kindred spirits turn up.
How to out-extreme them: "Humans are an incorrigible scourge on the fragile face of the Earth. The only solution is to all move to another, more resilient planet asap!"

**AFUN**

Organization: **AL-FIRQAT UN-NAAJIYAH (the Saviour Sect)**
Extreme beliefs: Would like to see the implementation of Sharia law in the UK – which under their rule would be known as the Islamic Republic of Great Britain. Sample article on website: "Kill those who insult the Prophet Muhammad".
How to join them: Any person can become a member of the Saviour Sect, providing they strictly adhere to the teachings of the Prophet Muhammad (SAW) and his Companions.
How to out-extreme them: N/A

**UKLL**

Organization: **UK LIFE LEAGUE**
Extreme beliefs: "We want to close [the abortion industry] down. Period. No compromise, no excuses. Killing a baby is always wrong. Abortion is murder." They request any information on "abortionists, clinic workers and anybody else who actively supports unborn child-killing".
How to join them: Contact the UKLL office for a Pro-Life Action pack: UK LifeLeague, 11 Waterloo Place, London, SWY 4AU.
How to out-extreme them: "Sperm are alive. Male masturbation should count as genocide!"

N.B.: Make sure you tell these organizations that you are also joining the other five this week!

# Jan 29–Feb 4

## Monday 29

## Tuesday 30

## Wednesday 31

## Thursday 1

## Friday 2

## Saturday 3

## Sunday 4

Join extremist organizations and out-extreme them

Monday 5

Tuesday 6

Wednesday 7

Thursday 8

Friday 9

Saturday 10

Sunday 11

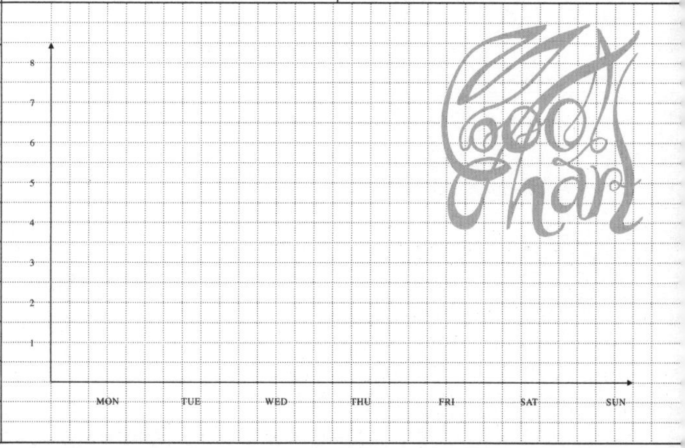

Leave your wallet on the street

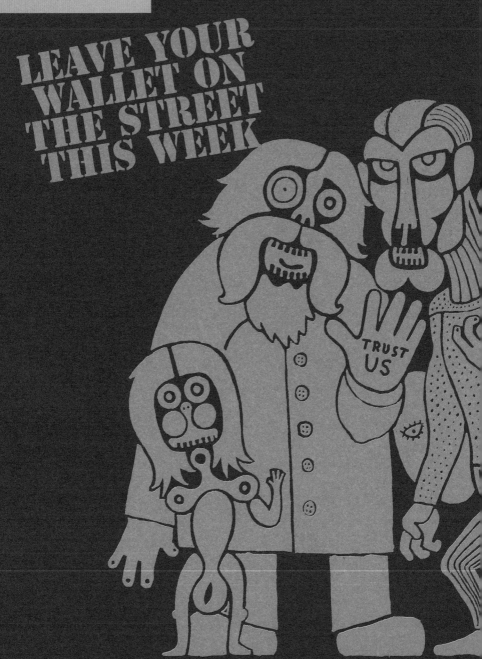

LEAVE YOUR WALLET ON THE STREET THIS WEEK

TRUST US

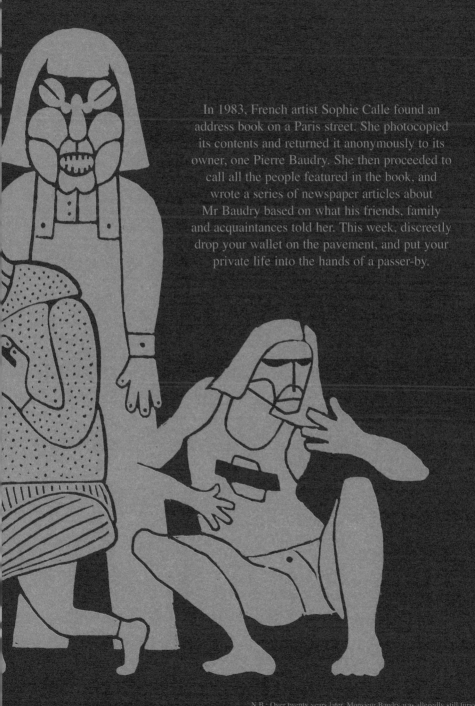

In 1983, French artist Sophie Calle found an
address book on a Paris street. She photocopied
its contents and returned it anonymously to its
owner, one Pierre Baudry. She then proceeded to
call all the people featured in the book, and
wrote a series of newspaper articles about
Mr Baudry based on what his friends, family
and acquaintances told her. This week, discreetly
drop your wallet on the pavement, and put your
private life into the hands of a passer-by.

N.B.: Over twenty years later, Monsieur Baudry was allegedly still furious.

# This week, pick a partner based on genetic superiority

Like any other animal, we must select our sexual partners on strict Darwinian grounds. So make sure your sexual mate is from the top of the gene pool, and if not, replace them; there is no room for losers in this harsh evolutionary race we call "love".

Monday:
Get two persons of the opposite sex to buy you a drink.*

Tuesday:
Tell your two admirers that it's your birthday, and see which one manages to find you a suitable present first.

Wednesday:
Discuss your future plans and assess which potential partner will be more solvent and/or caring for your offspring.

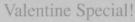

Valentine Special!

**Thursday:**
Women: get your suitors to compete for the privilege of moving your sofa from one room to the other. Men: get your suitresses to compete for the privilege of nursing you through a bout of "man-flu".

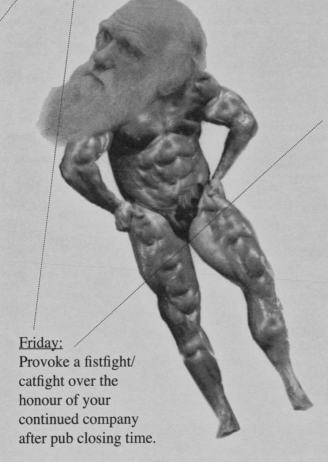

**Saturday:** Provoke a full-blown duel between your suitors, to the death if this is legal in your country.

**Sunday:**
Reward the glorious winner in bed with a little genetic pooling.

**Friday:**
Provoke a fistfight/ catfight over the honour of your continued company after pub closing time.

*Including your present partner if you have one. There's no reason why they should be exempt from the Darwinian test.

# February 12–18

## Monday 12

## Tuesday 13

## Wednesday 14

## Thursday 15

```
8
7
6
5
4
3
2
1
      MON    TUE    WED    THU    FRI    SAT    SUN
```

## Friday 16

## Saturday 17

## Sunday 18

Pick a partner based on genetic superiority

## February 19–25

| Monday 19 | Tuesday 20 | Wednesday 21 |
|---|---|---|
| | | |

| Thursday 22 | Friday 23 | Saturday 24 |
|---|---|---|
| | | |

Sunday 25

Draft your speech to the UN

# Draft your speech to the UN this week

## Hippie

Mr Secretary General, Mr President, distinguished guests, ladies and gentlemen:
Thank you for the privilege of being selected to speak as average representative of the human race.
I can't believe everyone on the planet is listening to this, all the millions and billions and trillions of you, I mean it kind of blows my mind. Every word that I say is beamed straight into the hearts of the whole wide world, and that is truly awesome.
I'm not an expert on the world's problems like all of you, I'm sure you know what you're doing. All I can offer is the people's perspective. What do the people want? Well, the people want peace, that's all. It's a beautiful word, it's a beautiful thing. It's what the world wants, it's what the world needs. In the words of another average Joe, "can't we all just get along?"
So please just keep that in mind as you debate geopolitical stuff.
And I just want to say one final thing, to the children… There is hope. We're doing this for you. We're going to make it better, and that's a promise. Peace.

Thank you.

## Paranoid

Mr Secretary General, Mr President, distinguished guests, ladies and gentlemen:
Thank you for the privilege of being selected to speak as average representative of the human race.
I know you're trying to switch on the mind-control device you've implanted in my brain, but it's not working you jackals! I'm wearing a thick magnetic copper helmet that blocks all gamma rays.
You can fool some people some of the time but you can't fool all the people most of the time.
I'm onto you guys, and don't think you can scare me with your UN death squads and your black helicopters. I used to be in 'Nam, and so I can hear choppers coming a mile away, medication or no medication! If any freedom-loving folks in the world are intercepting this transmission, please come and rescue me, I'm in the lair of the antichrist! Vade retro Satanas!
You won't take me alive, d'you hear!

Thank you.

Every year, the United Nations selects one average human being to make a speech alongside all the heads of state at the plenary meeting of the General Assembly in New York in September. This is your chance to influence the world! Draft your speech and send it to the UN (Office of the President of the General Assembly, United Nations, New York, NY 10017, USA). Here is a guide to the main types of speech, along with their likelihood of selection.

## Political

Chance of selection: 0/10

Mr Secretary General, Mr President, distinguished guests, ladies and gentlemen:
Thank you for the privilege of being selected to speak as average representative of the human race. It is high time that the human race had a voice here, for since the UN's founding, it has been nothing but a gentlemen's club for the world's fat cats, a transparent veneer on the global totalitarianism of the usual patriarchal élite. I am surprised that all of you here manage to keep a straight face as you pass resolution after resolution enforcing the status quo, and continue to despoil both the poor and the planet in the process.
You are indeed united, not for the world, but against it. If you had any shame, you would disband now and return to your countries to be lynched by your countrymen. Then we might start anew, and humankind might stand a chance.

Thank you.

## Alien

Chance of selection: 3/10

*Mr Secretary General, Mr President, distinguished guests, ladies and gentlemen: Thank you for the privilege of being selected to speak as representative of the alien race. I am Sdfbxtrftptt, Vice Emperor of Zorg. Do not be alarmed at my appearance, my tentacular genitalia are quite harmless unless aroused. I have come to announce the temporary annexation of your planet. We Zorgoids have nearly run out of plankton, which as you must know powers all warp-drive space travel technology. Your planet's oceans contain enough to last us three months, which isn't much, but is better than nothing. Anyway, we have begun scooping it up this morning. We will not harm you humans directly, but as plankton is the basis of your food chain, its removal will soon spell the end of life on earth, so we strongly suggest you come up with a replacement. You have three months, starting now. Thank you.

Shout
with joy,

then hug
the nearest
stranger

and tell them
you've just won
the lottery.

Feb 26–Mar 4

keep it up

for the rest
of the week
and see

how many new
friends you can
acquire.

## Monday 26

## Tuesday 27

## Wednesday 28

## Thursday 1

8
7
6
5
4
3
2
1

MON    TUE    WED    THU    FRI    SAT    SUN

## Friday 2

## Saturday 3

## Sunday 4

Tell everyone you've just won the lottery

Monday 5

Tuesday 6

Wednesday 7

Thursday 8

Friday 9

Saturday 10

Sunday 11

Only do things you have never done before

# This week, only do things you have never done before.

Only meet new people

Only wear new clothes

Only give to new beggars

Only think new thoughts

Only eat new food

Only read new books

www.
thiswebsite
willchangeyour
life.com

Only browse new websites

Only watch new channels

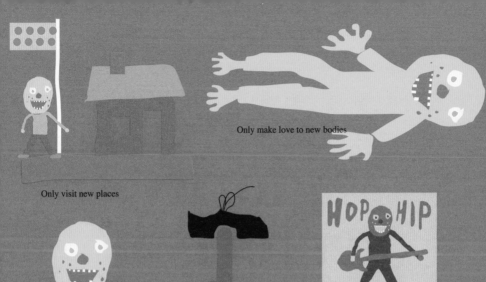

Only visit new places

Only make love to new bodies

Only dance new moves

Only buy new furniture

Only listen to new music

What happens if I put *sand* in my coffee instead of sugar? *Can* humans *drink* sand?

Only discuss new topics

Only dream new dreams

Only seek new thrills

Only whistle new tunes

Only kiss new faces

# This week, "glorify terrorism"

**Benrik readers in the UK are particularly lucky that an entirely new life-changing opportunity has recently presented itself. Thanks to the British state, "glorifying terrorism" can now land you in prison for years. This preposterously vague criminal offence is still in its infancy though, so help the courts decide what constitutes "glorification" by walking around with one of the following badges.**

TERRORISM GLORIFIER

I LOVE TERRORISM IT'S SO MACHO!

When I grow up, I want to be a terrorist!

**Badges and legal help available via www.thiswebsitewillchangeyourlife.com!**

## Monday 12

## Tuesday 13

## Wednesday 14

## Thursday 15

## Friday 16

## Saturday 17

## Sunday 18

"Glorify" terrorism

**Monday 19** St. Patrick's Day

**Tuesday 20**

**Wednesday 21**

**Thursday 22**

**Friday 23**

**Saturday 24**

**Sunday 25**

MON  TUE  WED  THU  FRI  SAT  SUN

Bribe people

# BRIBE PEOPLE ALL WEEK

£1

Supermarket
checkout girl to let
you jump the queue

£23

Airline hostess
to upgrade you to
business class

£10

Traffic warden
to tear up parking ticket

£14

Public bus
to detour via
your address

£18

Teacher
to give you
better grade

£59

Council to
pick up your
rubbish first

Bribing is an essential social practice, the lubricant in the engine of the free market, helping to bridge supply and demand. Other cultures know this, which is why they ignore misguided advice to abolish it. Good bribes, tactfully delivered, will guarantee you a more stress-free life in no time. Practise the art of bribery this week, starting with our rough guide to tariffs below.

Tube driver
to drive faster
than normal

Personal
trainer to go easy
on training

Lapdancer
to smile more
genuinely

Cable guy to
connect you to
forbidden channels

Government to
build nuclear power
plant in someone
else's back garden

Benrik to
include your photo
in next book

# This week, kill a commercial

TV advertising may indeed create unnecessary wants, but more crucially, most of it is patronizingly brain-dead. Commercials hold up a funfair mirror to society, leading us to conclude that people are stupider than in reality. By targeting the lowest common denominator, this cheerful garbage lowers collective self-esteem and quality of life, not to mention the average IQ. This week, Benrik readers are to join together, vote on the most insulting current commercial, and complain to get it taken off air. Visit www.thiswebsitewillchangeyourlife.com to vote in your country!

These are the relevant bodies to complain to. Write a calm, convincing letter outlining the reasons for your complaint, and explaining why the commercial is insulting your intelligence and should be banned forthwith. NB They usually receive a few dozen complaints at the most. Thousands will prove effective.

UK: Advertising Standards Authority, Mid City Place, 71 High Holborn, London WC1V 6QT
AUSTRALIA: The Advertising Standards Bureau, Level 2, 97 Northbourne Avenue, Turner ACT 2612
CANADA: Advertising Standards Canada, 175 Bloor Street East, South Tower, Suite 1801, Toronto, Ontario M4W 3R8
SOUTH AFRICA: Advertising Standards Authority, P.O. Box 41555, Craighall, Johannesburg 2024
NEW ZEALAND: Advertising Standards Complaints Board, P.O. Box 10675, Wellington
PORTUGAL: Instituto Civil da Autodisciplina da Publicidade (ICAP), R. Gregório Lopes, Lote 1515, Loja 6, 1400-408, Lisbon

WELLBEING INSURANCE
We care... because you do.

You've never tasted nuthing til you've tasted NUTTY NUTS!

SOUTHERN AIRLINES
Opening up the skies.

NEW RECORVE WITH POWER-STEERING
Give your life a new direction.

BRUTUS AFTERSHAVE
The Mark Of A Man.

GLOBAL NETWORKS
Putting you and the world ...together.
CRUNCHY POP CEREAL
It'll make your head go poppity-pop!
You'll be laughing all the way to the FIRST BOSTON BANK!

**Monday 26**

**Tuesday 27**

**Wednesday 28**

**Thursday 29**

| | MON | TUE | WED | THU | FRI | SAT | SUN |

**Friday 30**

**Saturday 31**

**Sunday 1**

Kill a commercial

## Monday 2

## Tuesday 3

## Wednesday 4

## Thursday 5

## Friday 6

Good Friday

## Saturday 7

## Sunday 8

Easter Sunday

Enter Miss or Mr World

# This week, enter Miss or Mr World

Miss World and its male counterpart Mr World are eagerly-awaited global events, on a par with the Olympics or the World Cup. The reason for their appeal? They don't just focus on the competitors' appearance, but also on their inner beauty. There is thus no reason why you shouldn't stand a good chance of winning, provided your personality is in good shape. Apply to Miss World Organization, enclosing a photo.

Photo

Dear organizers,

Please include me in your selection process for Miss World/
Mr World 2007. I believe I deserve to win because:
.................................................................................
.................................................................................
.................................................................................
.................................................................................
.................................................................................
.................................................................................
.................................................................................
.................................................................................
.................................................................................

Name:..........................................................................
Address:......................................................................
Date of birth:..............................................................
Height:.........................................................................
Statistics:....................................................................
Occupation:................................................................
Dream:.........................................................................
Hobbies:......................................................................

I support world peace          ☐
I don't support world peace    ☐

The Virgin Mary in an apple

The Virgin Mary in a vegetarian lasagne

The Virgin Mary in a beard

# This week, claim to see the Virgin Mary in an everyday object

The Virgin Mary in tea leaves

The Virgin Mary in a bar of soap

The Virgin Mary in a CD-ROM

The Virgin Mary in a cloud

This is an easy task, as evidenced by the numerous people who already do it every year. With a bit of imagination and creative effort, the Virgin Mary can be seen in a wide range of settings. Draw inspiration from these examples to create a plausible likeness. Call the Vatican, alert the media, set up a shrine and charge the impressionable faithful an admission fee. If people doubt you, overcome them with your faith by screaming "Do you see it? Do you see it?" at the top of your voice until they admit they do.

Email the Vatican: benedictxvi@vatican.va

The Virgin Mary in a wolverine

The Virgin Mary in a church

# April 9–15

## Monday 9 — Easter Monday

## Tuesday 10

## Wednesday 11

## Thursday 12

MOOD CHART

8
7
6
5
4
3
2
1

MON    TUE    WED    THU    FRI    SAT    SUN

## Friday 13

## Saturday 14

## Sunday 15

Claim to see the Virgin Mary in an everyday object

| Monday 16 | Bank Holiday (Scotland) | Tuesday 17 | Wednesday 18 |
|---|---|---|---|

| Thursday 19 | Friday 20 | Saturday 21 |
|---|---|---|

Sunday 22

8
7
6
5
4
3
2
1

MON    TUE    WED    THU    FRI    SAT    SUN

Have a nervous breakdown

# THIS WEEK HAVE A NERVOUS BREAK DOWN

The gnawing stress that underlies modern
capitalism means that regular nervous
breakdowns are inevitable for all of us.
Don't wait until yours hits you: precipitate
it this week using the triggers below, and
emerge from treatment a stronger person.

MONDAY
• Set your alarm clock early.
• Chainsmoke from the moment you get out of bed.
• Skip breakfast.
• Drink espressos all day.
• Commute at the height of rush-hour.
• Keep an eye on the 24-hour breaking-news channels.
• Watch the stock markets.
• Sit in meetings.
• Question your boss's decisions.
• Call automated customer helplines.
• Get drunk.
• Work through the night.

TUESDAY
• Book yourself into a psychiatric
institution for the rest of the week
and enjoy your breakdown!

# This week, help finish roadworks

**XXXXX**
Obsolete Mains Water
**REMOVE**

**REWIRE**
**URGENT!**

**EXCLUSION ZONE**

**CRIME SCENE!**
Call Police Infrastructure Team 0978 654 555 before tampering

**OBSTRUCTION IN PIPE**
Bore in with pneumatic drill at 30°.

**Dept of Works Study**
078-0002

Engineer-in-charge: B. McConnell

Move all pipes 60" deeper and 20" to the left

Roadworks are a constant source of frustration to city dwellers. No sooner is one hole filled than another is dug, often in the very same place, and left unmanned for days. This week, speed matters along: find a hole where no work seems to be proceeding. Stick one or several of the messages below on pipes, barriers or other infrastructure where you judge they may bring works to a swifter conclusion.

# TREATED WASTE
## HAZCHEM RISK 0

# Work Complete
## Passed/Approved ☒
**Fill in site immediately**

◀ **CONNECT PIPES TO EACH OTHER** ▶

PRIORITY B-1

NATIONAL GRID
240V
USE GLOVES!

CAUTION!
HOT

## Monday 23

## Tuesday 24

## Wednesday 25

## Thursday 26

MON   TUE   WED   THU   FRI   SAT   SUN

## Friday 27

## Saturday 28

## Sunday 29

Help finish roadworks

## Monday 30

## Tuesday 1

## Wednesday 2

## Thursday 3

## Friday 4

## Saturday 5

## Sunday 6

MOOD CHART

MON    TUE    WED    THU    FRI    SAT    SUN

Golden Bookmark Week

# Benrik Golden Bookmark Week!

Benrik have inserted a Golden Bookmark into one
Diary this year! If you are the lucky reader who finds
it in his or her copy, you get to set this week's task and
order all the other readers around. Ask them to repaint
your bathroom. Ask them to carry you everywhere.
Ask them to beat up your creditors. Ask them whatever
takes your fancy. This week, you rule Benrikland.

Everyone else: your task this week is to do whatever
the Golden Bookmark finder says, as notified on
www.thiswebsitewillchangeyourlife.com.

**Benrik Golden Bookmark!**
Congratulations, reader! You have
found Benrik's Golden Bookmark.
This bookmark was hidden in one
and only one copy of This Diary Will
Change Your Life 2007. It entitles
you to set the life-changing task that
Benrik's dozens of thousands of other
readers must follow for one week!
Date: Week of April 30 to May 6

## Benrik's Taupe Bookmark!

Communications reader! You have
found Benrik's Taupe Bookmark.
This bookmark was hidden in one
and only one copy of *This Diary Will
Change Your Life 2007*. It means you
must follow whatever life-changing
task Benrik's dreamt of thousands of
other readers set you this week...

Date: Week of April 30 to May 6.

# Benrik's Taupe Bookmark!

If you have found Benrik's Taupe Bookmark,
then sadly everyone else is allowed to order
you around this week. Please report to
www.thiswebsitewillchangeyourlife.com
so people can boss you about.

Benrik
Collective
Task

# This week, demonstrate in favour of the government!

Is it any wonder our leaders take so little notice of demonstrations when they are so predictably anti-governmental? Countries such as China and North Korea show that public protest need not be antagonistic. The state is only human after all: it responds to positive feedback much more than to petty-minded criticism. This week, engage in mass rallies to encourage your government in its actions and spur it on to greater things.

Report to www.thiswebsitewillchangeyourlife.com to coordinate demos worldwide!

GOOD LUCK WITH YOUR POLICIES!

DOWN WITH THE OPPONENTS OF THE STATE!

IMPLEMENT
**THE
LAW!**

**THE RIOT
POLICE
RULES!**

**THE PACE
OF REFORM
IS GOOD!**

**TERMINATE
THE ENEMIES
OF THE PRIME
MINISTER!**

**UP WITH THE
GOVERNMENT!**

**NO TO
NAY-
SAYERS!**

Monday 7　　　　　Bank Holiday (UK)

Tuesday 8

Wednesday 9

Thursday 10

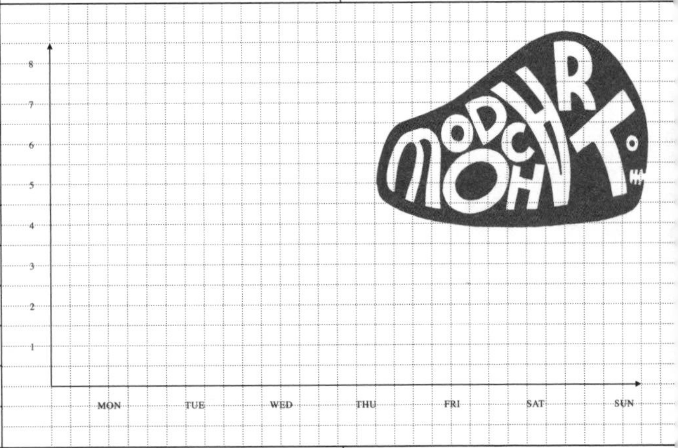

Friday 11

Saturday 12

Sunday 13

Demonstrate in favour of the government

| Monday 14 | Tuesday 15 | Wednesday 16 |
|---|---|---|
| | | |

| Thursday 17 | Friday 18 | Saturday 19 |
|---|---|---|
| | | |

Sunday 20

MON TUE WED THU FRI SAT SUN

Smile inappropriately

# This week, smile inappropriately

"Sick of smiling appropriately? Who tells you when to smile anyway? Corporate advertisers for the great toothpaste market are making millions from linking normal life with appropriate smiling everyday. So today disrupt their marketing ploys by smiling when you shouldn't. Smile when you hear bad news. Smile when you hear something offensive. Smile when a baby cries. Just smile, and smile and smile your face off, but only when you shouldn't. Let them make a marketing campaign of that. You will either be applauded for being enigmatic or they will just incarcerate you for being a psychopath. And if they do, just smile."

# Positive Discrimination Week

Don't speak to
anyone wearing
orange.

Avoid men
with excessive
nostril hair.

No physical
contact with bald
people.

Don't answer
any questions from
brunettes.

Accept sexual offers
only from people born
in the countryside.

Only do
business with people
taller than you.

Run away
screaming from
anyone pregnant.

Refuse to smile
back at pony-tailed
checkout girls.

Ask any neighbour
with green curtains
to move.

Tell your
children to avoid
cat-owners.

Denounce
left-handers
to the police.

Give money
to beggars with
green eyes only.

Only buy
from women
over 56.

Refuse to
shake hands with
electric-razor users.

Verbally
abuse men with
size 7 feet.

Torture
anyone with
freckles.

Discrimination is not necessarily evil, as long as you discriminate in a totally arbitrary manner. Treating people equally is a recipe for permanent boredom. Make everyone's life more lively this week by obeying these simple rules.

Refuse to slow-dance with 30 to 39-year-olds.

If anyone under 55 kgs enters the room, leave.

Ignore people who mispronounce the word "aluminium".

Brutalize anyone you catch eating between meals.

If a redhead appears on screen, switch off your TV.

Ask for your money back if your taxi driver's hair is curly.

Don't go into any shop run by a couple.

Chase anyone with high blood pressure out of town.

Don't sit down next to anyone with myopia.

Blame cardigan-wearers for a political problem.

Don't allow 42-year-olds into your home.

Fire employees with "outie" belly buttons.

Only employ people with glasses.

Flirt only with people whose name begins with K.

Ostracize opera-goers.

Stone anyone who doesn't own this book.

# May 21–27

## Monday 21

## Tuesday 22

## Wednesday 23

## Thursday 24

## Friday 25

## Saturday 26

## Sunday 27

Positive Discrimination Week

| Monday 28 | Bank Holiday (UK) | Tuesday 29 | Wednesday 30 |
|---|---|---|---|

| Thursday 31 | Friday 1 | Saturday 2 |
|---|---|---|

Sunday 3

Groom someone on the net

# This week groom someone on the net

*Internet grooming* is a potent new psychological tool, which has been unfairly misappropriated by paedophiles. You don't have to be a twisted sicko to use it; anyone may *groom* anyone else for a wide variety of useful tasks, from teaching you a foreign language to polishing your shoes. Follow the basic guidelines below and report your grooming successes this week on www.thiswebsitewillchangeyourlife.com.

The seven stages of grooming

## 1. Find a chat room
There are hundreds of thousands of chat rooms on the internet. Try and find one that corresponds to your particular interest e.g. if you wish to groom someone to trim your hedge, you might try chatting on www.gardenchat.com.

## 2. Select a groomee
Observe the chat before intervening. Is there anyone no one is talking to? Is anyone clearly new to the group and looking for a chatting companion? If their nickname (or *handle*) includes the word *lonely*, you have a groomee.

## 3. Introduce yourself
Take care not to scare your groomee away by declaring your grooming interest prematurely. <Hi>, <Hello>, <Wazzup> are all effective introductions. <Any1 wanna walk my dog round the blck every morning?> is not.

## 4. Sympathize with their problems
Befriend your groomee by encouraging them to share their problems. Are they fed up with their job? Is their partner cheating on them? Are they feeling a little depressed? You may not give a damn, but it creates a useful bond between you.

## 5. Share secrets
Deepen the bond by trusting your groomee with some secrets. This is the critical phase. Start with uncontroversial secrets like <I feel worthless inside> and gradually link them to your interest e.g. <Maybe I'd feel better if my bathroom was retiled>.

## 6. Meet up
After grooming them for the best part of a week, ask them to meet up; by now, they should trust you. That's no reason to trust them, however, as the internet is full of weirdos. Make sure you tell a friend where you're going, and when you mean to return.

## 7. Reap the rewards!
If you have groomed them properly, your groomee should be primed to do your bidding. Sit back as they follow your orders to tidy up your garage, shampoo your carpet, teach you blackjack, or whatever on earth it is you have groomed them to do.

*I've been
made
redundant*
Support ☐
Betrayal ☐

*Actually,
I was fired*
Support ☐
Betrayal ☐

*I was fired
for stealing*
Support ☐
Betrayal ☐

*I stole to pay
for my heroin
habit*
Support ☐
Betrayal ☐

*I've been
"using" for
years now*
Support ☐
Betrayal ☐

*I normally sell
my body to get
the money*
Support ☐
Betrayal ☐

**Stages of disgrace**
(Reveal the extent of your disgrace
gradually, noting whether they
support you at each stage)

June 4–10

# *Disgrace Week*

This week, tell everyone you've lost your job, home
and place in society, and see who still talks to you.
When the chips are down, who are your real friends?

But I caught
genital herpes
as a result
Support ☐
Betrayal ☐

My partner
has kicked
me out
Support ☐
Betrayal ☐

My family have
disowned me
Support ☐
Betrayal ☐

The police
are looking
for me
Support ☐
Betrayal ☐

I'm totally
bankrupt
Support ☐
Betrayal ☐

Can I stay at
your place for
a while?
Betrayal ☐

# June 4–10

## Monday 4

## Tuesday 5

## Wednesday 6

## Thursday 7

MON    TUE    WED    THU    FRI    SAT    SUN

## Friday 8

## Saturday 9

## Sunday 10

Disgrace Week

| Monday 11 | Tuesday 12 | Wednesday 13 |
|-----------|------------|--------------|

| Thursday 14 | Friday 15 | Saturday 16 |
|-------------|-----------|-------------|

Sunday 17

MOOD CHART

8
7
6
5
4
3
2
1

MON    TUE    WED    THU    FRI    SAT    SUN

Follow your body clock

June 11–17

# This week, follow your body clock

When the Lilliputians discovered Gulliver's watch, they surmised it was his God, as he did nothing without consulting it. And indeed one of the harshest constraints on our freedom is this unquestioning obedience to the hours, minutes and seconds. This week, let your body clock take over. Ditch all time-measuring devices, switch off your alarms and see how well your innate sense of time-keeping guides you. Lunch when you feel it's lunchtime. Sleep when you feel it's bedtime. Wake naturally. Don't ask what the time is, and you'll free yourself from its relentless march.

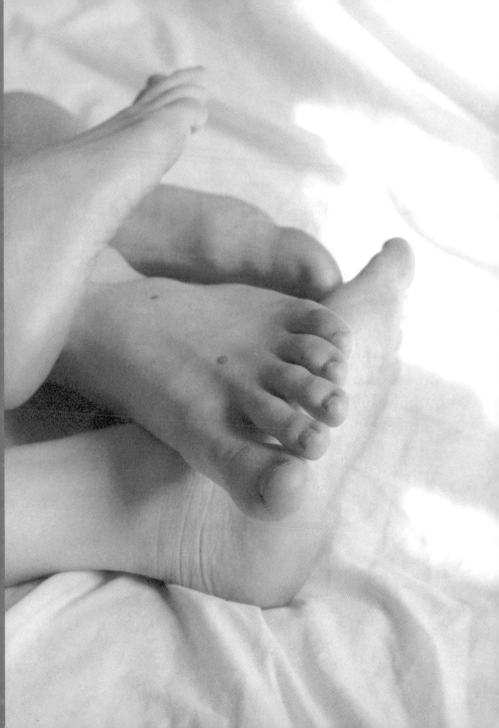

# This week, swap blood with another Benrik reader

Benrik readers are drawn together by a common mystical bond, a shared understanding of the world and a deep respect for the principles of extreme life-change. Make that bond sacred this week, by exchanging blood with another reader, and thus forging a lifelong kinship. Here is how:

1. Locate another Benrik reader. You may know one already, or you may find one through www.thiswebsitewillchangeyourlife.com.
2. Enquire if they are interested in becoming your sacred blood brother for all of eternity. If they decline, try not to take it personally.
3. Prick your thumb with a sterilized razor blade or needle (using a rusty knife is no longer considered essential).
4. Deposit some of your blood in a small sealable container. Again, don't go overboard: you don't need half a pint, just a few drops.
5. Seal tightly, affix the label provided, and mail to your soon-to-be Benrik blood brother. Allow three weeks for delivery.
6. When you receive your blood brother's sample, soak a swab in it, and carefully rub it into an open wound.
7. Before you do that, however, have it thoroughly screened for HIV and other blood-borne pathogens. You never know these days.
8. As you rub their blood into yours, chant some ancient Native American incantations, and voilà: you are now blood brothers, congratulations!

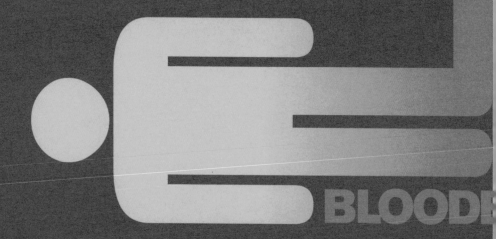

**BLOOD SAMPLE**

Name:..............................................................

Date of birth:...............................................

Gender:..........................................................

Blood group:.................................................

<u>Attention HM Customs:</u> This blood sample is due to be used for ritual purposes. It has no commercial value and is NOT subject to tax. Please pass it on without delay.

Affix this label on the container

# June 18–24

| Monday 18 | Tuesday 19 | Wednesday 20 |
|---|---|---|
| | | |

## Thursday 21

Friday 22 | Saturday 23 | Sunday 24

Swap blood with another Benrik reader

Monday 25

Tuesday 26

Wednesday 27

Thursday 28

Friday 29

Saturday 30

Sunday 1

8
7
6
5
4
3
2
1

MON    TUE    WED    THU    FRI    SAT    SUN

# GATECRASH THE NEWS THIS WEEK

**CATEGORY OF NEWS EVENT:**
*Political assassination*

Apologize for the murder on behalf of your government, saying it was due to a typing mistake.

**CATEGORY OF NEWS EVENT:**
*Natural disaster*

Enlist survivors and file a class action lawsuit against God and his representatives on earth, the Vatican.

**CATEGORY OF NEWS EVENT:**
*Terrorist threat*

Conduct your own interrogations, torturing suspicious passers-by until they confess their guilt or innocence.

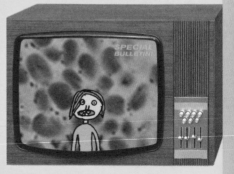

**CATEGORY OF NEWS EVENT:**
*Medical breakthrough*

Denounce the breakthrough as a fraud, and insist that they test it on your own body, in public.

This week, make your life immediately more exciting by going to the heart of the news. Switch on your TV, find out the number one event in the world, the biggest story on the planet, call your travel agent and get yourself over there immediately. *What to do when you get there:* since you're in the area, why not try to get on the world news yourself? The media are always hungry for a good story, even if it's not 100% verified.

In April 2002, Japanese backpackers Yuki Makano and Mina Takahashi strolled towards the Church of the Nativity in Bethlehem, totally unaware of the ongoing bloody siege between Israeli soldiers and Palestinian gunmen. As journalists and residents stared on bemused, the couple wandered around, guidebook in hand, and casually took in the sights. They were eventually rescued and told of the siege. "We have been on the road for six months and haven't watched television or read the newspapers", said Mr Makano.

CATEGORY OF NEWS EVENT: *Military invasion* — Broker a ceasefire by wandering across the battlefield with a large white flag.

CATEGORY OF NEWS EVENT: *Celebrity break-up* — Claim it's because of the secret affairs you've been having with both the celebrities.

CATEGORY OF NEWS EVENT: *Sporting competition* — Wait for the final day and streak across the ground at the very last, crucial minute.

CATEGORY OF NEWS EVENT: *Accidental thermonuclear explosion* — Even if you manage to find transportation to this event, you are permitted not to go if you prefer.

**MSH mail – New Message**

To: System Administrator

Cc:

Bcc:

Subject: RE: MAKE YOUR PENIS HUGE!!!

Dear Sir,

Thank you very much for the offer to MAKE YOUR PENIS HUGE!!!
I am gratified that you should contact me personally with your "AMAZING DEAL". I have been despairing of my less-than-huge appendage for years now, along with my wife and past girlfriends. "NEED A LONG DONG?" summarizes my dilemma succintly. That is why I am minded to accept your offer. Your "OR YOUR MONEY BACK!" guarantee seems particularly advantageous. It would be an unreasonable consumer indeed who did not take you up on it. Please send me your "XTRA LARGE PACKAGE" forthwith (in its discreet brown envelope). Again, thanks ever so for your email. I look forward to hearing from you on any forthcoming promotions.

Yours sincerely,

☐ Copy Message to Sent Folder

Done

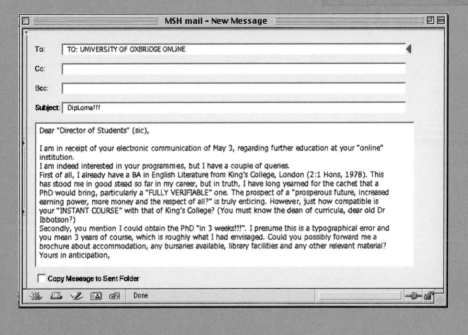

**MSH mail – New Message**

**To:** TO: UNIVERSITY OF OXBRIDGE ONLINE

**Cc:**

**Bcc:**

**Subject:** DipLoma!!!

Dear "Director of Students" (sic),

I am in receipt of your electronic communication of May 3, regarding further education at your "online" institution.
I am indeed interested in your programmes, but I have a couple of queries.
First of all, I already have a BA in English Literature from King's College, London (2:1 Hons, 1978). This has stood me in good stead so far in my career, but in truth, I have long yearned for the cachet that a PhD would bring, particularly a "FULLY VERIFIABLE" one. The prospect of a "prosperous future, increased earning power, more money and the respect of all?" is truly enticing. However, just how compatible is your "INSTANT COURSE" with that of King's College? (You must know the dean of curricula, dear old Dr Ibbotson?)
Secondly, you mention I could obtain the PhD "in 3 weeks!!!". I presume this is a typographical error and you mean 3 years of course, which is roughly what I had envisaged. Could you possibly forward me a brochure about accommodation, any bursaries available, library facilities and any other relevant material?
Yours in anticipation,

☐ Copy Message to Sent Folder

Done

**MSH mail – New Message**

**To:** ml09880@freenet.tz

**Cc:**

**Bcc:**

**Subject:** Re: SIERA LEONE Orphan

Dear Yolanda,
I was truly sorry to hear of the tragic deaths of your father and your "senior brothers" at the hands of the rebel troops. Civil war is a blight on the face of Africa, and we must all keep up the pressure on politicians to end it. In some ways you are more fortunate than most though. The 18.9 million dollar fortune that your father left you from his "import/export agricultural supplies and tooling" business is a boon, which will enable you to rebuild your life and start again, full of hope. Of course I am willing to help you with the bank account, but I won't hear a word about being paid to do so! I am simply glad to help. My details are: Barclays account number 67657689, sort code 13-66-08. Let me know your details and I will wire over the $55,000 for the local death duties.

Looking forward to meeting you when you get your visa! I have a daughter your age, who also loves to "surf" the internet!
XXX

☐ Copy Message to Sent Folder

Done

# July 2–8

## Monday 2

## Tuesday 3

## Wednesday 4

## Thursday 5

## Friday 6

## Saturday 7

## Sunday 8

Answer spam emails

| Monday 9 | Tuesday 10 | Wednesday 11 |
|---|---|---|

| Thursday 12 | Friday 13 | Saturday 14 |
|---|---|---|

Sunday 15

MON  TUE  WED  THU  FRI  SAT  SUN

Wear a burka

# WEAR
# A BURKA
# ALL WEEK

Amidst the Western hysteria about various Islamic customs, find out for yourself what it is like to move about society covered from head to toe. Observe people's reactions. Witness their prejudices. Monitor your own sense of body and self, as you walk around conspicuous yet invisible. Revise your view of life accordingly.

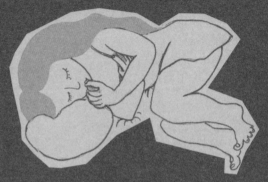

# THIS WEEK, SLEEP IN PUBLIC

Sleeping in public is usually the prerogative of winos and the homeless. This week, however, you too are to sleep outside your comfort zone. Find a nice park bench, a comfortable bus stop, or someone's front garden, and settle down for the night. Trust others to respect your sleep. And to encourage them, hang this sign around your neck as you slumber.

BENRIK PUBLIC SLEEPING WEEK

# DO
# NOT
# DISTURB!

**Dear passer-by,**
I am sleeping here for a while.
You are a fellow human being,
and so I trust you to leave me in
peace and not to hurt, dispossess
or abuse me in any way. You may
watch over me though if you like.
I apologize for any snoring.

# July 16–22

## Monday 16

## Tuesday 17

## Wednesday 18

## Thursday 19

MOOD CHART

| | | | | | | |
|---|---|---|---|---|---|---|
| MON | TUE | WED | THU | FRI | SAT | SUN |

## Friday 20

## Saturday 21

## Sunday 22

Sleep in public

| Monday 23 | Tuesday 24 | Wednesday 25 |
|---|---|---|
| | | |

| Thursday 26 | Friday 27 | Saturday 28 |
|---|---|---|
| | | |

Sunday 29

MOOD CHART

| | MON | TUE | WED | THU | FRI | SAT | SUN |
|---|---|---|---|---|---|---|---|

Check that your sex life is normal

# This week, check that your sex life is normal

We get most of our information about what constitutes a normal sex life from the media. But *Cosmo* and Hollywood are hardly the most reliable guides to what goes on in real bedrooms. This week, overcome your coyness: fill in this questionnaire and ask your peer group to assess how much you deviate from the sexual straight and narrow.

## Sum up your sexual life:

**VIRGINITY**
Lost? Yes ☐ No ☐
At age:.......................................................
To:..............................................................

**NUMBER OF PARTNERS**
One (self) ☐
One (other) ☐
Several (number):......................................

**INTERCOURSE**
Regular? Yes ☐ No ☐
Frequency:......per day/week/month/year
With:...........................................................
....................................................................
....................................................................
....................................................................
....................................................................

**FANTASIES**
Favourite:..................................................................................................................
....................................................................................................................................
Secret:.......................................................................................................................
....................................................................................................................................
Repressed:.................................................................................................................
....................................................................................................................................

**FETISH**
Legal:........................................................................................................................
....................................................................................................................................
Illegal:.......................................................................................................................
....................................................................................................................................
Law doesn't even acknowledge it:..........................................................................

**VENEREAL DISEASES**
None                    ☐
Embarrassing            ☐
Life-threatening        ☐

## Ask your friends for their opinion:

| FRIEND'S NAME | FRIEND'S VERDICT ON YOUR SEX LIFE |
|---|---|
| 1 | Normal ☐ Boring ☐ Perverted ☐ Friendship terminated ☐ |
| 2 | Normal ☐ Boring ☐ Perverted ☐ Friendship terminated ☐ |
| 3 | Normal ☐ Boring ☐ Perverted ☐ Friendship terminated ☐ |
| 4 | Normal ☐ Boring ☐ Perverted ☐ Friendship terminated ☐ |
| 5 | Normal ☐ Boring ☐ Perverted ☐ Friendship terminated ☐ |
| 6 | Normal ☐ Boring ☐ Perverted ☐ Friendship terminated ☐ |
| 7 | Normal ☐ Boring ☐ Perverted ☐ Friendship terminated ☐ |
| 8 | Normal ☐ Boring ☐ Perverted ☐ Friendship terminated ☐ |
| 9 | Normal ☐ Boring ☐ Perverted ☐ Friendship terminated ☐ |
| 10 | Normal ☐ Boring ☐ Perverted ☐ Friendship terminated ☐ |
| 11 | Normal ☐ Boring ☐ Perverted ☐ Friendship terminated ☐ |
| 12 | Normal ☐ Boring ☐ Perverted ☐ Friendship terminated ☐ |
| 13 | Normal ☐ Boring ☐ Perverted ☐ Friendship terminated ☐ |
| 14 | Normal ☐ Boring ☐ Perverted ☐ Friendship terminated ☐ |
| 15 | Normal ☐ Boring ☐ Perverted ☐ Friendship terminated ☐ |
| 16 | Normal ☐ Boring ☐ Perverted ☐ Friendship terminated ☐ |
| 17 | Normal ☐ Boring ☐ Perverted ☐ Friendship terminated ☐ |
| 18 | Normal ☐ Boring ☐ Perverted ☐ Friendship terminated ☐ |
| 19 | Normal ☐ Boring ☐ Perverted ☐ Friendship terminated ☐ |
| 20 | Normal ☐ Boring ☐ Perverted ☐ Friendship terminated ☐ |
| 21 | Normal ☐ Boring ☐ Perverted ☐ Friendship terminated ☐ |
| 22 | Normal ☐ Boring ☐ Perverted ☐ Friendship terminated ☐ |
| 23 | Normal ☐ Boring ☐ Perverted ☐ Friendship terminated ☐ |
| 24 | Normal ☐ Boring ☐ Perverted ☐ Friendship terminated ☐ |
| 25 | Normal ☐ Boring ☐ Perverted ☐ Friendship terminated ☐ |
| 26 | Normal ☐ Boring ☐ Perverted ☐ Friendship terminated ☐ |
| 27 | Normal ☐ Boring ☐ Perverted ☐ Friendship terminated ☐ |
| 28 | Normal ☐ Boring ☐ Perverted ☐ Friendship terminated ☐ |
| 29 | Normal ☐ Boring ☐ Perverted ☐ Friendship terminated ☐ |
| 30 | Normal ☐ Boring ☐ Perverted ☐ Friendship terminated ☐ |

# This week everyone invade Svankær

Svankær is a small isolated Danish village in Jutland with an ageing population of 300. In an average year, it may see 50 tourists. This week, the dozens of thousands of Benrik followers are asked to assemble there to take it over and impose Benrik Rule. This will serve as a mere prelude to Benrik's eventual takeover of a much larger administrative unit, and in due course the world.

# Benrik Rule

#1 Benrik followers to set up roadblocks in and out of village and cut phone lines
#2 Benrik followers to be billeted into villagers' houses (three per room max.)
#3 Benrik themselves to move into local manor house
#4 Locals to all memorize *This Diary Will Change Your Life* by heart
#5 Benrik followers to buy up all the village's food every morning at 7 a.m.
#6 Reverse curfew: no one allowed out before 11 a.m. (except to carry out Rule 5)
#7 Benrik followers have right to deflower first-borns of local peasantry and livestock
#8 Benrik followers to commandeer local church for trials of locals who resist
#9 Benrik followers to drink grog out of resisting locals' severed heads
#10 Benrik followers to tidy everything up as it was, before leaving on Sunday

Fly in to Aalborg Airport. Take the train from Hamburg. Drive from Aaarhus,
taking the E45 turn-off signposted Mors. Land at Thylom off the ferry.
Careless talk costs lives! If anyone visits Svankær before July 30, 2007,
please do not show them these pages, as it would ruin the surprise entirely.

## Jul 30–Aug 5

### Monday 30

### Tuesday 31

### Wednesday 1

### Thursday 2

### Friday 3

### Saturday 4

### Sunday 5

Everyone invade the Danish village of Svankær

Monday 6

Tuesday 7

Wednesday 8

Thursday 9

Friday 10

Saturday 11

Sunday 12

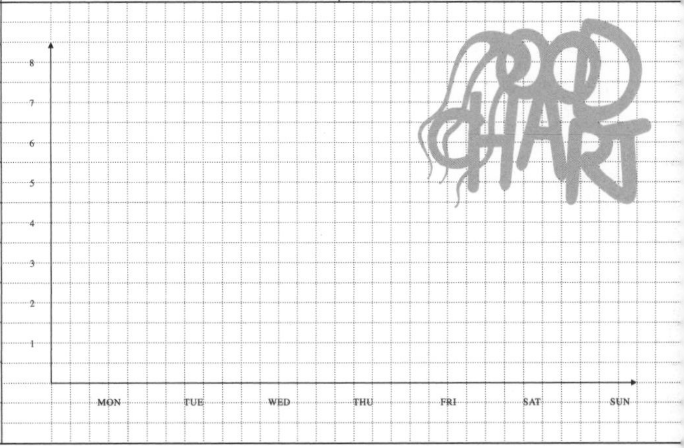

POP CHART

8

7

6

5

4

3

2

1

MON   TUE   WED   THU   FRI   SAT   SUN

Opt out of the internet

# This week, opt out of the internet

It is a cliché to point out just how much electronic data is being collected about us. From surveillance CCTV cameras to electronic banking, from supermarket loyalty schemes to internet service-provider logs, there is hardly any aspect of our lives that isn't monitored by someone somewhere. If the current trends continue, we are told, we will end up with a police state.

What many fail to realize, however, is that it is already too late. Your privacy is only protected by the limits of the technology: all this information is currently stored in disparate locations. But as processing power expands and databases are increasingly interconnected, we are heading for the emergence of a unified computer record of all the current information about you; this is the future of the internet.

For an authoritarian government of the future, it will be child's play to search your file automatically, and convict you retrospectively for anything you have said or done today. What may seem innocuous now, may be regarded as subversive in twenty years' time. It is therefore quite possibly too late to save yourself, but you can at least try

## Wipe the record

Erase any blogs you have written. Delete any message-board posts. Unsubscribe from any email lists. Cancel your credit cards. Never google again. Try to cancel your virtual presence.

## Confuse the database

Already today, software looks for recognizable patterns to help categorize you. Prevent them from pinning you down: invest in weapons stocks one minute, and give to a landmine charity the next.

## Change your name

A unique name makes it easier to track you down: there aren't that many "Archibald Dokins" about. Change your name by deed poll to something common, like "Sam Brown", to help cover your electronic tracks.

## Burn this book

Ownership of anti-state instructions may in itself constitute an offence in the future. Burn this book, and ask the bookshop you bought it from to delete your transaction from its records.

# This week, do something that passers-by will never forget

Do something surreal and unwordly, something that will give others an experience they will remember for the rest of their lives, a break in the mundanity of their existence, a moment of poetry that they will recall on their deathbed as they drift away with a chuckle...

Pour a cappuccino into your shoe

Throw away a banana and eat the peel

Threaten a traffic warden with a traffic cone

Release fish fingers back into the sea

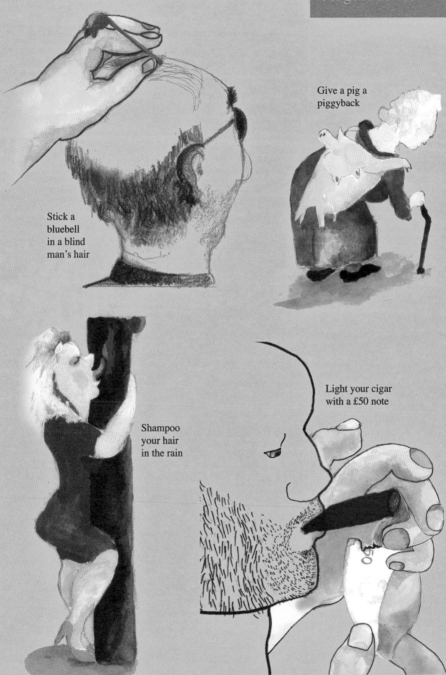

Stick a
bluebell
in a blind
man's hair

Give a pig a
piggyback

Shampoo
your hair
in the rain

Light your cigar
with a £50 note

**Monday 13**

**Tuesday 14**

**Wednesday 15**

**Thursday 16**

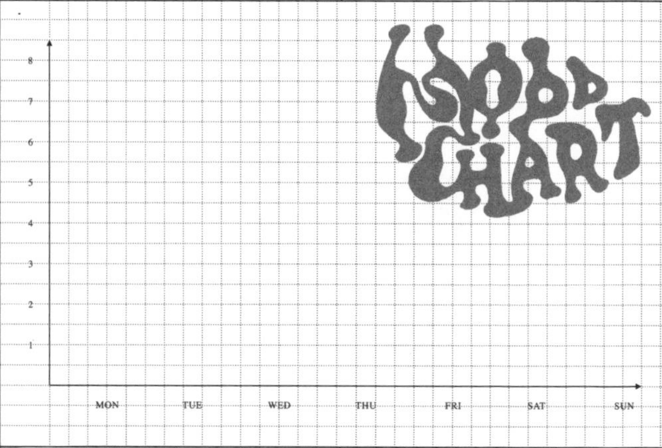

MOOD CHART

MON    TUE    WED    THU    FRI    SAT    SUN

**Friday 17**

**Saturday 18**

**Sunday 19**

Do something that passers-by will never forget

Monday 20

Tuesday 21

Wednesday 22

Thursday 23

Friday 24

Saturday 25

Sunday 26

CHART

8
7
6
5
4
3
2
1

MON    TUE    WED    THU    FRI    SAT    SUN

Advise your military

# This week, advise your military

## Sample letters

Private D. Fordham
3rd Battalion
7th Armoured Brigade
Basra
Iraq

Dear Private,

Your country misses you and is appreciative of your dedication and commitment to protecting us and preserving our hard-won freedoms. Keep up the good work, soldier! Now, may I be so bold as to offer you some free advice? From what I can tell on the news, the city of Kerbala looks relatively undefended at the moment. If you crept up through the eastern suburbs in the dead of night with a few other sound chaps from your platoon, I bet you could bag yourself some "insurgents".

A grateful citizen,
.....................

Sgt. Myers
25th Infantry Division
Camp Anaconda
Uruzgan
Afghanistan

Dear Sergeant,

Your efforts abroad help us all. Please know that we support all that you do to protect millions of people. As you've probably been informed, the Taliban are regrouping in the Waziristan region. My research indicates that if you and your unit hit them hard with 81mm mortar fire tonight at 23.00, you stand a good chance of smashing them to smithereens!
Coordinates are: N31° 30' 49.10 " E65° 51' 39.80 ".
Let me know how it goes.
Good luck!

A citizen-soldier,
.....................

The armed forces of Western powers are currently deployed across the globe in a variety of combat missions. It is your duty not only to support them, but to provide them with any tactical insights you have gleaned from your personal study of the battlefield. Write to someone in your national military directly this week, and claim your rightful place in the chain of command.

Lieutenant R. McGregor
9th Armoured Brigade
SFOR
Sarajevo
Bosnia

Dear Lieutenant,

My thoughts are with you during this difficult time away from loved ones. Your actions are making peace possible throughout the world. Now, I spend a lot of time on internet chat rooms, and I've picked up rumours of potential civil unrest in Macedonia. You could cross the border with 3rd Battalion at dawn, and take control of the major strategic centres including TV stations. I'll square it with your superiors at this end. God bless you and your men.

With you all the way!
…………………

General J. Beckbridge
Middle East Tactical Command
C/JTF-KU (Fwd)
Camp Doha
Kuwait

Dear General,

I just wanted to say how much I appreciate all that the armed forces do to protect freedom around the globe. You do a great job and are well worth my tax money. I have a mission for you. I'm guessing the Iranians are hiding some nukes in the Khuzestan region. The element of surprise is on our side. Orders are to invade it immediately with a blitzkrieg pincer movement from Iraq and Qatar, with 42 Commando spearheading the operation and the 1st Armoured Division bringing up the rear. Start asap.

Carpe diem and all that,
…………………

# Subliminal Week

This week, Benrik will be changing your life in your sleep. Simply download the *"Subliminal Life-Changing Podcast"* from www.thiswebsitewillchangeyourlife.com, and fall asleep to it every night this week. We do not want to divulge the ways in which your life will change, but let's just say you will be amazed by the results! Monitor the changes below.

"Subliminal Life-Changing Podcast"

| Changes | Monday | Tuesday |
|---|---|---|
| Changes in everyday behaviour | | |
| Changes in sexual behaviour | | |
| Changes in political views | | |
| Changes in religious outlook | | |
| Changes in basic personality | | |
| Changes in physical appearance | | |
| Changes in hormonal levels | | |
| Changes observed by work colleagues | | |
| Changes observed by family members | | |
| Changes observed by children | | |
| Changes observed by doctor | | |
| Changes observed by media | | |
| Changes in blood group | | |
| Changes in DNA | | |

# Instructions

Download the Podcast from www.thiswebsitewillchangeyourlife.com/podcast
as an mp3 file. Save it to your desktop. Either listen to it from your computer,
or burn it as a CD, or use an mp3 player. The Podcast lasts 45 minutes, with a 15
minute blank at the beginning to allow you to fall asleep. If you wake up before
the Podcast is finished, Benrik will not be responsible for any brain damage.

| Wednesday | Thursday | Friday | Saturday | Sunday |
|-----------|----------|--------|----------|--------|
|           |          |        |          |        |
|           |          |        |          |        |
|           |          |        |          |        |
|           |          |        |          |        |
|           |          |        |          |        |
|           |          |        |          |        |
|           |          |        |          |        |
|           |          |        |          |        |
|           |          |        |          |        |
|           |          |        |          |        |
|           |          |        |          |        |
|           |          |        |          |        |
|           |          |        |          |        |

Warning: Do NOT listen to the Benrik Subliminal Life-Changing Podcast whilst awake and conscious. The Podcast is based on
neurolinguistic programming targeted specifically at your subconscious. It will not work if you listen to it on a conscious level.
And in fact you will develop a subconscious resistance to its messages which will destroy its effectiveness entirely.

# Aug 27–Sept 2

**Monday 27**  Bank Holiday (England and Ireland)

**Tuesday 28**

**Wednesday 29**

**Thursday 30**

8
7
6
5
4
3
2
1

MON    TUE    WED    THU    FRI    SAT    SUN

**Friday 31**

**Saturday 1**

**Sunday 2**

Subliminal Week

## Monday 3

## Tuesday 4

## Wednesday 5

## Thursday 6

## Friday 7

## Saturday 8

## Sunday 9

Switch on your appendix

# This week switch on your appendix

The human appendix is generally dismissed by the medical profession as a vestigial organ, that is, an organ that was once useful but is now obsolete in evolutionary terms. Conventional wisdom holds that it only merits our attention when it becomes inflamed to the point where it must be removed. This is a short-sighted view. There is another school of thought: the appendix may be beginning its evolutionary journey, gradually growing into an organ with new capacities that we can scarcely yet imagine, such as telepathy, or the ability to digest Martian foodstuffs. This week, try turning your appendix on and triggering these new and wonderful functions.

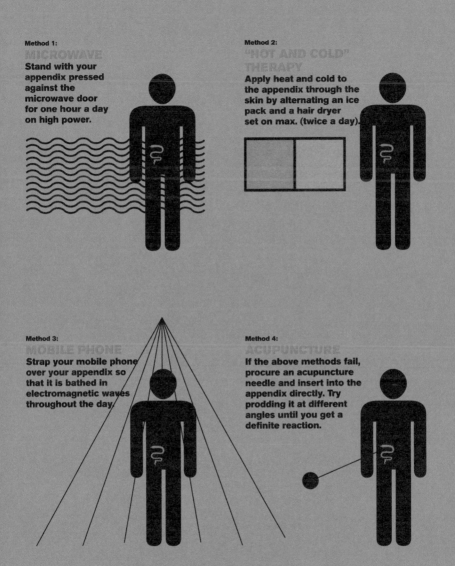

**Method 1:**

MICROWAVE

Stand with your appendix pressed against the microwave door for one hour a day on high power.

**Method 2:**

"HOT AND COLD" THERAPY

Apply heat and cold to the appendix through the skin by alternating an ice pack and a hair dryer set on max. (twice a day).

**Method 3:**

MOBILE PHONE

Strap your mobile phone over your appendix so that it is bathed in electromagnetic waves throughout the day.

**Method 4:**

ACUPUNCTURE

If the above methods fail, procure an acupuncture needle and insert into the appendix directly. Try prodding it at different angles until you get a definite reaction.

REFERENCES: Collins, D.C. (1955) "A study of 50,000 specimens of the human vermiform appendix." Surg Gynecol Obstet. 101: 437–445.
Saave, J. J. (1955) "Absence of the vermiform appendix; report of a case discovered at necropsy." Acta Anat (Basel). 23: 327–329.
Iuchtman, M. (1993) "Autoamputation of appendix and the 'absent' appendix." Arch Surg. 128: 600.
Dasso, J. F., Obiakor, H., Bach, H., Anderson, A. O., and Mage, R. G. (2000) "A morphological and immunohistological study of the human and rabbit appendix for comparison with the avian bursa." Dev Comp Immunol 24: 797–814.

In restaurants, finish
other people's leftovers

Read newspapers and books
over other people's shoulders

# Parasite Week

In our intricate society, there are
many opportunities for freeloading.
This week, see if you can live literally
at the expense of others.

Smell other people's perfume

Enjoy the conversations of complete strangers

Listen to the radio on someone else's set

# September 10–16

## Monday 10

## Tuesday 11

## Wednesday 12

## Thursday 13

## Friday 14

## Saturday 15

## Sunday 16

| Monday 17 Bank Holiday (Scotland) | Tuesday 18 | Wednesday 19 |
|---|---|---|

| Thursday 20 | Friday 21 | Saturday 22 |
|---|---|---|

Sunday 23

CHART

See a dead body

# See a dead body this week

This may seem gruesome, but how can you hope to understand your mortality if you have never come face to face with death? This week, make arrangements to view a corpse, and reflect on the fleetingness of life.

## VIEWING ETIQUETTE

The deceased deserve respect. To arrange a viewing, contact your local funeral director in writing, outlining your reasons and asking for the permission of the bereaved relatives. Stress that you will not interfere with the funeral arrangements and offer to make a small donation to a charity of the family's choice. At the viewing: remain silent, try to control your emotions and of course do not attempt to take photographs. Afterwards, go outside, take a deep breath of fresh air and enjoy life to the full while you can.

Made me reflect ☐
Didn't make me reflect ☐

# START A BUSINESS EMPIRE FROM YOUR GARAGE

The business world is packed with billionaires who started off in their garage. The products they sell are usually perfectly mundane – the garage is the key, as it will give your business empire that homespun authenticity that consumers demand these days. To help you gain valuable PR, you will also need some likely story about how your Mum brewed coffee all night long to keep you going. Here are some examples of business empires that can be started by practically anyone.

PR angle: "The founder's 6-year-old sister stuffed a banana skin in the blender as a joke. The rest is history…"

PR angle: "Ricky got the idea when his toaster broke. Everyone liked the half-toasted sandwiches better. So Ricky kept on makin' them!"

PR angle: "My buddies and I were always going on about how good Britney must smell up close, so I thought, hey that's a great business idea!"

PR angle: "My gran started forgetting things, so I said to myself, why not come up with an enzyme-powered ionic silicon interface and plug it right smack into her parietal lobe?"*

* Starting this particular empire may require a) that you drop out of your PhD in surgical nanotechnology and b) a fairly big garage.

The first "Diary Will Change Your Life" was hand-lithographed using potato prints in Ben's garage back in 2003. Ben and Henrik hawked it around boot sales in vain for weeks, until one magic day, their big corporate publisher organized a promotional radio and print marketing multi-media campaign, helping them to achieve that crucial word-of-mouth crossover tipping point. They haven't looked back since.

# September 24–30

## Monday 24

## Tuesday 25

## Wednesday 26

## Thursday 27

MOOD CHART

8
7
6
5
4
3
2
1

MON    TUE    WED    THU    FRI    SAT    SUN

## Friday 28

## Saturday 29

## Sunday 30

Start a business empire from your garage

**Monday 1**

**Tuesday 2**

**Wednesday 3**

**Thursday 4**

**Friday 5**

**Saturday 6**

**Sunday 7**

MON    TUE    WED    THU    FRI    SAT    SUN

Monopolize radio phone-ins

# Monopolize radio phone-ins this week

Radio stations love phone-ins because they're a cheap way of filling airtime. You love them because they're a golden opportunity to charm the nation. Call a different talk show every hour this week, and impress listeners all over the country with your wit, insight and irresistible personality. By Sunday, you should aim to have become a much-loved national figure, with offers pouring in for your very own show.

Media training in 3 easy steps:
1) Before going live, you will be put through to a junior researcher who will want to check that you have something relatively sane to say. Once you are on air, don't feel obliged to stick to it of course.
2) Listeners will be busy doing the ironing, driving to work and generally getting on with their lives. To lodge yourself in their consciousness, you will need an original angle: the prime minister has an evil twin, perhaps, or the national lottery is a money-laundering front.
3) Every great media personality needs a memorable catchphrase, that kids will repeat in the playground and bores will repeat in the pub. "Nice to see you, to see you nice" is memorable. "Am I on air yet?" is not. Try to sign off dramatically as well, although not by slamming the phone down, which soon grows tiresome.

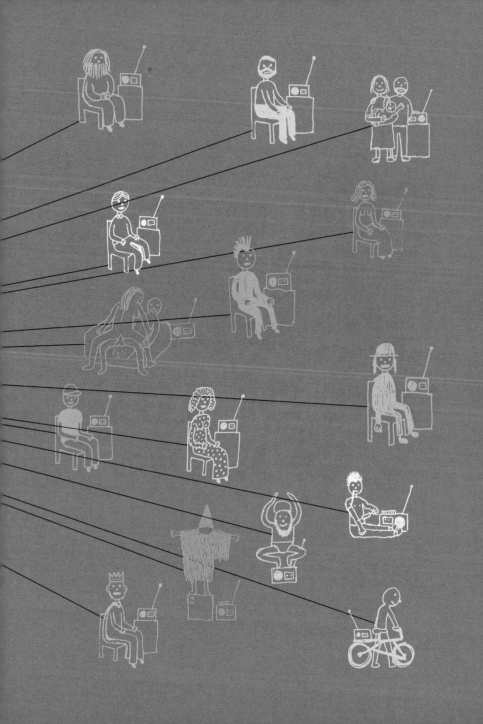

# This week, let the skeletons out of your closet

Sexual skeletons:

...........................................
...........................................
...........................................
...........................................

Relationship skeletons:

...........................................
...........................................
...........................................
...........................................

Professional skeletons:

...........................................
...........................................
...........................................
...........................................

**Everyone has at least one thing in their past that they would hate to see come out. If you have lived to the full, you probably have several. This week, Benrik declare an amnesty: write down your shameful hidden past on this page, and present it to those around you. Secrets will out – better your loved ones find out this way than through their own devices.**

Criminal skeletons:

.......................................

.......................................

.......................................

.......................................

Childhood skeletons:

.......................................

.......................................

.......................................

.......................................

Miscellaneous skeletons:

.......................................

.......................................

.......................................

.......................................

Benrik note: Let He Who Is Without Sin Cast The First Stone (The Bible)

# October 8–14

**Monday 8**

**Tuesday 9**

**Wednesday 10**

**Thursday 11**

**Friday 12**

**Saturday 13**

**Sunday 14**

Let the skeletons out of your closet

Monday 15

Tuesday 16

Wednesday 17

Thursday 18

Friday 19

Saturday 20

Sunday 21

MON TUE WED THU FRI SAT SUN

Go on hunger strike

# This week, go on hunger strike

Contrary to popular perception, you don't have to be famous or in the news to go on hunger strike. In fact, when the hunger strike was invented (by the Celts), it was mostly used to help settle local disputes such as the recovery of debts. The procedure is to notify whoever you are hunger-striking against, sit in front of their door, and fast until they grant you redress. If they let you starve to death, they suffer social disgrace, and face compensation claims by your family. Hunger strikes are easy to organize, non-violent and inexpensive, yet psychologically intimidating. Embark on one for the week, and settle whatever dispute is currently ruining your peace of mind.

Health & Safety: as long as you only fast for a week, you shouldn't suffer irreversible damage; death normally occurs around

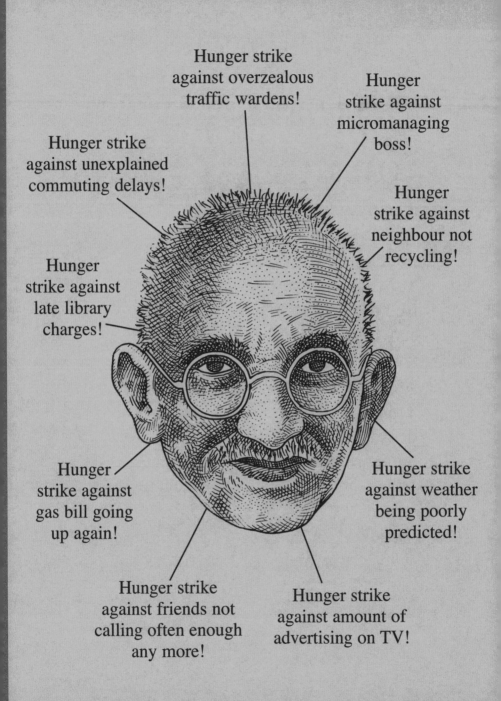

Hunger strike against overzealous traffic wardens!

Hunger strike against micromanaging boss!

Hunger strike against unexplained commuting delays!

Hunger strike against neighbour not recycling!

Hunger strike against late library charges!

Hunger strike against gas bill going up again!

Hunger strike against weather being poorly predicted!

Hunger strike against friends not calling often enough any more!

Hunger strike against amount of advertising on TV!

the 60-day mark. Consult your doctor before starting a hunger strike, particularly if you are elderly or infirm. Good luck.

# THIS WEEK, DIG A TUNNEL TO THE OTHER SIDE OF THE WORLD

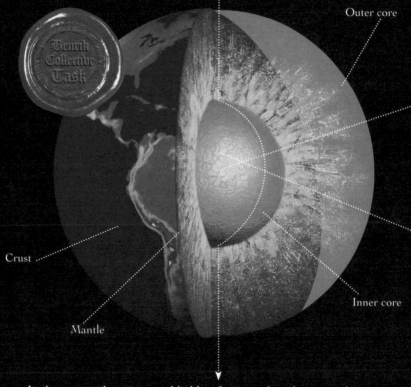

Outer core

Crust

Mantle

Inner core

In the race to the stars, mankind has forgotten its other great dream: digging straight through to the other side of the Earth. This week, Benrik are launching a renewed attempt to achieve this tremendous goal by asking their readers to dig a tunnel right through the Earth. If every single person reading this spends a minute or two digging, the tunnel will be finished in no time. To your spades! Note: the Earth's inner core is made of very dense solid matter, so whoever gets to it first will have to dig around it.

Digging location #1: 22 Bethnal Green Road, London, United Kingdom

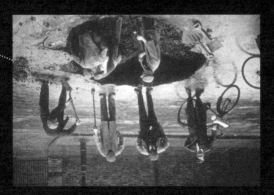

Digging location #2: 458 Springfield Rd, Sydney, Australia

YOU MAY START DIGGING WHEREVER YOU ARE IN THE WORLD, OF COURSE, BUT ON YOUR OWN IT WILL TAKE LONGER.

## Monday 22

## Tuesday 23

## Wednesday 24

## Thursday 25

MOOD CHART

| | | | | | | |
|MON|TUE|WED|THU|FRI|SAT|SUN|

8
7
6
5
4
3
2
1

## Friday 26

## Saturday 27

## Sunday 28

Dig a tunnel to the other side of the world

| Monday 29 | Tuesday 30 | Wednesday 31 |
|---|---|---|
| | | |

| Thursday 1 | Friday 2 | Saturday 3 |
|---|---|---|
| | | |

Sunday 4

Send your DNA to the authorities

# This week, send your DNA to the authorities

These days, it is only too easy for an innocent citizen to get mixed up in some global security scare by mistake. You may be in the wrong place at the wrong time. Or an acquaintance may mention you under torture. Or the computer may have you confused with someone with a similar name. Before you know it, you're off to an interrogation camp in the middle of nowhere for five years! Avoid such difficulties by volunteering your DNA ahead of time. Send it to the world's leading security services, and they'll be able to check you off their "suspects" lists early on in any investigation, for guaranteed peace of mind. Here is where to send your DNA. Careful! Each security service has its preferred form of DNA. Make sure you send the right one to avoid complications.

## FBI

Preferred DNA format:

### lock of hair

Dear FBI,
Please record my DNA and check my name off your "most wanted" list. Thank you.

Signed.............................................................

Address...........................................................

Send to: Federal Bureau of Investigation, J. Edgar Hoover Building, 935 Pennsylvania Avenue, NW, Washington, D.C. 20535-0001, USA

## CIA

Preferred DNA format:

### swab of saliva

Dear CIA,
I'm innocent! But here's my DNA anyway, just so you can be 100% sure. Good luck.

Signed.............................................................

Address...........................................................

Send to: Central Intelligence Agency, c/o Office of Public Affairs, Washington, D.C. 20505, USA

Preferred DNA format:

## vial of blood

Dear FSB,
Just in case you were suspecting me, I'm sending you my DNA so you can rule me out of your investigations. Bye for now.

Signed..................................................................

Address................................................................

Send to: FSB, 1/3 Bolshaya Lubyanka Ul., 101000, Moscow, Russia

---

Preferred DNA format:

## urine sample

Dear MI5,
I'm a law-abiding citizen. I have nothing to fear, now or in the future. Here's my DNA for safe storage.

Signed..................................................................

Address................................................................

Send to: MI5, Thames House, Millbank, PO Box 3255, London SW1P 1AE, UK

---

## Interpol

DNA format:

## toenail cuttings

Interpol,
so much crime being
national these days, you
be too careful. Check my
and cross me off your list!

............................................................

............................................................

Interpol General Secretariat, 200,
arles de Gaulle, 69006 Lyon, France

---

## MSS

Preferred DNA format:

## small jar of earwax

Dear Ministry of State Security,
I doubt I am on your list of suspects, but just in case, here's my DNA to prove my innocence.

Signed..................................................................

Address................................................................

Send to: Ministry of State Security,
14 Dongchang'an Street, Doncheng District, Beijing, China

# Become spokesperson for
# your neighbourhood this week

A strong and united local community can help defeat crime, littering, loneliness and other modern social vices. Bring your neighbourhood together this week: stick a sign in your front window that speaks up on its behalf.

Anyone
bringing
property prices
down will be
expelled from
this postcode.

This
neighbourhood
is free of
Ukrainians,
and that's how
we all like it.

By
Neighbourhood
Watch Order:
all house
lights off at
11.30 p.m.

THIS local neighbourhood says: stop the kerb-crawling!

The people who live below enjoy extra loud sex on Saturday mornings (9 a.m.)

We don't like strangers round these parts…

Welcome to the more upmarket end of the street by far.

This neighbourhood castrates burglars on sight. You have been warned.

## Monday 5

## Tuesday 6

## Wednesday 7

## Thursday 8

MOOD CHART

8
7
6
5
4
3
2
1

MON  TUE  WED  THU  FRI  SAT  SUN

## Friday 9

## Saturday 10

## Sunday 11

Become spokesperson for your neighbourhood

**Monday 12**

**Tuesday 13**

**Wednesday 14**

**Thursday 15**

**Friday 16**

**Saturday 17**

**Sunday 18**

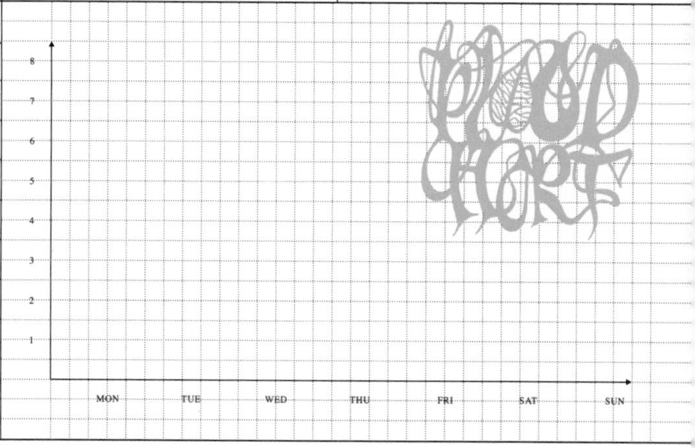

8
7
6
5
4
3
2
1

MON    TUE    WED    THU    FRI    SAT    SUN

Hug every tree you walk past

This week,
hug every
tree you
walk past

"Daisy"
Oak
21 years old
New Forest, UK

"Fiona"
Sycamore
7 years old
Primrose Hill
London, UK

"George"
Chestnut
59 years old
Botanic Gardens
Adelaide, Australia

"Margaret"
Willow
28 years old
Suffolk St
Birmingham, UK

"Sebastian"
Beech
17 years old
Paparoa National Park
South Island, New
Zealand

"Stacy"
Pine
36 years old
Black Forest, Germany

Tree-hugging is a well-attested life-enhancing practice, that brings you closer to nature and helps you reconnect with your very own "roots". This week, hug every single tree you encounter for at least one minute. Most trees are highly huggable, but here are the world's most affectionate ones; look out for them.

"Michael"
Pine
68 years old
Richmond Park
London, UK

"Bob"
Cypress
Age: unknown
Lincoln Park Golf
Course
San Francisco, USA

"Betty"
Poplar
12 years old
20 miles east of Durban on the R102
Kwazulu-Natal, South Africa

"Keanu"
Coconut
23 years old
Garden of Mr/Mrs Dale
33 Woodlawn Drive
Honolulu, Hawaii, USA

"Mitsuko"
Bonsai (careful not to crush it)
49 years old
1-1-20 Kanayama Cho Naka Ku
Nagoya, Japan

"Hjalmar"
Christmas
5 years old
Erstavik-skogen
Sweden

Etiquette: it is considered bad form to carve your name in the tree you have just hugged.

# THIS WEEK, ERECT A STATUE OF YOURSELF IN A PUBLIC PLACE

Statues are a short cut to immortality. Contact an affordable local sculptor this week and have them cast your features in the material of your choice. As soon as it's ready, choose a public space where your statue will look right at home; a large square perhaps, or a park. Everyone knows that's where statues belong, so as long as you install it with confidence, you won't be challenged. Finally, don't forget the plaque with your name, date of birth, and public achievements; tourists require this kind of information.

SIDNEY KENTMAN
PANEL-BEATER
1954–

# November 19–25

## Monday 19

## Tuesday 20

## Wednesday 21

## Thursday 22

MON  TUE  WED  THU  FRI  SAT  SUN

## Friday 23

## Saturday 24

## Sunday 25

Erect a statue of yourself in a public place

Monday 26

Tuesday 27

Wednesday 28

Thursday 29

Friday 30

Saturday 1

Sunday 2

MOOD CHART

8

7

6

5

4

3

2

1

MON TUE WED THU FRI SAT SUN

Increase your pain threshold

# This week, increase your pain threshold

What doesn't kill you makes you stronger. This week, gradually increase the level of pain you can cope with, so that you won't get hurt by what life throws at you.

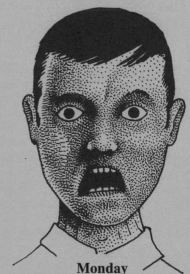

**Monday**
Ask an acquaintance
to pinch your arm
for 5 minutes

**Tuesday**
Get someone to
pull your hair hard
for 10 minutes

**Wednesday**
Stand under an
ice-cold shower
for 15 minutes

**Thursday**
Ask a trusted friend
to spank you until
you plead for mercy

**Friday**
Pour the hot wax
of two candles onto
your bare skin

**Saturday**
Convince a dentist to
remove a back tooth
without anaesthetic

**Sunday**
Ask the love of
your life to break
your heart

Pain gets a bad press, but it is crucial to our survival. Pain alerts our body to danger and enables us to avoid long-term damage. Indeed, people who can't feel pain at all are usually dead by 30. If none of the exercises suggested here cause you any pain, stay indoors for the rest of your days if you value your life.

# BEFRIEND A CUSTOMER CARE PERSON

Customer-care hotlines recruit individuals with exceptional emotional intelligence and empathy, who are well worth having as friends. This week, make it your mission to befriend a customer-carer and meet them for real by the end of the week.

**DAY 1**
Call a customer-care line with an obscure question that they can't answer immediately. Make sure you get the customer-carer's name and agree to call them back. E.g. *Hello! What do you call the exact shade of green you use on your biscuit packaging, as I want the same for my curtains?*

**DAY 2**
Ring back the next day, asking to speak to the same person. As they give you the information you requested, change the question slightly, to prolong the contact. E.g. *You're going to laugh, but I've just remembered I'm allergic to green, what about the blue?*

**DAY 3**
When you next speak, introduce some emotional tension into your relationship. Being so empathetic, they will start to sympathize. E.g. *My house has just burnt down, so I don't need any damn curtains! What am I going to do? Oh mercy on me!*

**DAY 4**
Call them back the next day to thank them for being so empathetic, and apologize for selfishly only talking about yourself all the time. E.g. *It turned out to be a false alarm, but I was in such distress and you saved me! And you must have so many problems of your own!*

**DAY 5**
Personalize the relationship. You've been through a lot together over the last few days. Get him or her to acknowledge the bond between you. E.g. *This may sound crazy, but I feel some connection between us that goes way beyond biscuits. Are you a Gemini?*

**DAY 6**
Work out where the call centre is based, and wait for your customer-care friend to emerge. A fiver to the security guard will ensure they point out the right person. Don't say anything at this point, but follow them discreetly to find out where they live.

**DAY 7**
Knock on their door just before Sunday lunch, and introduce yourself. Carry a recording of your conversations to jog their memory. Hey presto! You have a new friend. E.g. *Surprise! I say, you're even lovelier in real life than you are on the phone. And look, I've brought you some biscuits!*

Some hotlines to get you started:
PG Tips 0800 454 611
Kelloggs 0800 626 066
McVities 0500 011 710
Boots 0800 915 0004
Cadbury 0800 559 3271
Walkers 0800 274 7777
Heinz 0800 496 3283
Durex 0800 338 739
Procter & Gamble 0800 085 0367
Lemsip 0500 455 456

## December 3–9

**Monday 3**

**Tuesday 4**

**Wednesday 5**

**Thursday 6**

**Friday 7**

**Saturday 8**

**Sunday 9**

Befriend a customer-care person

Monday 10

Tuesday 11

Wednesday 12

Thursday 13

Friday 14

Saturday 15

Sunday 16

| | | | | | | |
|---|---|---|---|---|---|---|
| 8 | | | | | | |
| 7 | | | | | | |
| 6 | | | | | | |
| 5 | | | | | | |
| 4 | | | | | | |
| 3 | | | | | | |
| 2 | | | | | | |
| 1 | | | | | | |
| MON | TUE | WED | THU | FRI | SAT | SUN |

Walk into a police station and announce you're giving yourself up

December 10–16

This Monday morning walk into a police station,

# announce you're finally giving yourself up and refuse to say another word for the rest of the week.

## Know your rights!

You may be giving yourself up, but that doesn't mean you're giving up your basic rights. Make sure the police follow due process, and if not, complain about it to the Independent Police Complaints Commission on 08453 002 002.

ARREST: An arrest is only lawful if you are told that you are under arrest and are given the grounds for your arrest at the time or as soon as possible afterwards. Once in custody, you are entitled to a clean cell with adequate heating, lighting and bedding, as well as access to toilet facilities.

DETENTION: The police must determine as soon as practicable whether there is enough evidence to charge you. They may only detain you for up to 36 hours without charge, unless you are lucky enough to be detained under recent anti-terrorist legislation, in which case it's 28 days.

SEARCH: If you refuse to identify yourself, a police officer of the same sex may search you for any clues. Strip searches are only allowed if the custody officer considers it to be strictly necessary, or if you specifically request one.

LEGAL ADVICE: Upon your arrest, you should be informed of your statutory right to consult a solicitor free of charge and in private. You can always exercise this right without actually speaking to the solicitor when they turn up of course.

RIGHT TO SILENCE: You have the right to silence. In the UK, however, it has been curtailed in recent years. Before, you were allowed to stay silent although anything you said could be held against you. Now, saying nothing may actually harm your defence.

USE OF FORCE: The police are allowed to use reasonable force where you refuse to consent to certain procedures, including fingerprinting and "non-intimate samples". However they may not use force to obtain "intimate samples", such as blood, semen or any tissue taken from an orifice other than the mouth.

USE OF TORTURE: The police are not really allowed to torture you, unless you are following this week's task in a dictatorial regime, which we do not recommend even in the name of extreme life-change.

RELEASE: The police may attempt to release you before the full week is up. They may for instance be tempted to deny there is enough evidence to suspect you of an actual offence. Foil their plan by rolling your eyes, dribbling, and making violent stabbing gestures. This should renew their interest.

# THIS WEEK, ADOPT A CHRISTMAS TURKEY

One surefire way of changing your life, and of doing good into the bargain, is to adopt a turkey destined for the Christmas pot. Contact Bernard Matthews on 01603 872611 and request that they spare your turkey's life. You will need to compensate them for the financial loss, and collect your adopted turkey within two days from their farm in Norfolk. The turkey may initially be traumatized, but with your patient love and care, it will in time recover, and reward you with its everlasting loyalty.

Caring for your turkey: Keep your turkey in a fenced-in yard, with plenty of room to exercise ($10m^2$ min). Domestic turkeys cannot fly, unlike their wild cousins, but you will still need to provide a roof for shelter. The best flooring for them is a dirt floor covered with hay, which you will need to change every couple of days. You should feed your turkey pet-shop pellets, although they will eat anything from grapes to acorns. The turkey is a companionable animal, so if possible you should adopt two. The male turkey is called a gobbler, the female is called a hen. Domestic turkeys are no longer capable of breeding naturally and will need your assistance: you will first need to milk the gobbler, then artificially inseminate the hen. Pregnancy lasts about 28 days, yielding a litter of "poults", which make a delicious starter lightly grilled with asparagus.

Monday 17

Tuesday 18

Wednesday 19

Thursday 20

| | MON | TUE | WED | THU | FRI | SAT | SUN |

Friday 21

Saturday 22

Sunday 23

Adopt a Christmas turkey

## Monday 24

## Tuesday 25
Christmas Day

## Wednesday 26
Boxing Day

## Thursday 27

## Friday 28

## Saturday 29

## Sunday 30

Doomsday Week: Prepare for the impending apocalypse due on Monday 31

# DOOMSDAY WEEK

## PREPARE FOR THE IMPENDING APOCALYPSE

Civilization is a fragile and precarious construct, a palace made of matchsticks that could easily collapse under the weight of a natural or manmade cataclysm. If it does end up annihilating itself, the remnants of humankind will have to somehow survive in the wreckage. Proficiency in database management won't get you very far in the fight for food, shelter and water. This week, practise elementary survival skills, so you can rebuild civilization from scratch if need be. This task won't just change your life: it could very well save it.

## LIGHTING A FIRE

Find a dry flat piece of softwood, and cut a groove down the middle. Find a strong thin length of hardwood, and run it back and forth down the groove, producing tinder that will eventually catch fire.

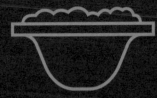

PRACTISE

## BUILDING A SHELTER

Find a natural depression in the ground, preferably dry and sheltered from the wind. Place large branches over it, then stack up smaller branches followed by turf and leaves.

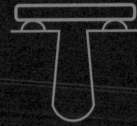

PRACTISE

## HUNTING

Dig a hole which is wider at the bottom than at the top. Cover it with a piece of wood placed on two stones. Mice and voles will seek cover there and fall in the hole, which they cannot climb out of.

PRACTISE

## FINDING WATER

Dig a hole in the ground, place a container inside the hole, and cover it with plastic. Water will condense during the night and drip into the container.

PRACTISE

## FISHING

Build a wall of sticks across a shallow stream, to divert fish into a trap, where you can use a movable stick net to keep and grab them as and when you require.

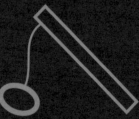

PRACTISE

## MAKING A WEAPON

Find a piece of hardwood about 40cm in length, and a suitably-shaped stone. Lash the stone and tie the lashing to the wood: you now have a lethal sling club. Gradually recreate civilization from hereon, until you reach annihilation again. Repeat.

# Lifeplanner

Plan your life from 0 to 100! From your choice
of cot to your choice of coffin, there are a million
decisions to be made. Get your life in order here.

| | | | | |
|---|---|---|---|---|
| 1 _Crucial formative influences_ | 11 | 21 | 31 _Settle down_ | 41 |
| 2 | 12 _Puberty (girls)_ | 22 _End of youthful illusions_ | 32 | 42 |
| 3 | 13 _Puberty (boys)_ | 23 | 33 | 43 |
| 4 | 14 _First cigarette behind bike shed_ | 24 | 34 | 44 _Midlife crisis_ |
| 5 | 15 | 25 | 35 _Itch (seven year-)_ | 45 _Take up golf_ |
| 6 | 16 _Exams_ | 26 | 36 | 46 |
| 7 | 17 | 27 | 37 | 47 |
| 8 | 18 _Drink legally_ | 28 _Marriage and mortgage_ | 38 | 48 |
| 9 | 19 | 29 | 39 | 49 |
| 10 | 20 | 30 _Party_ | 40 _Party_ | 50 _Party_ |

| | | | | |
|---|---|---|---|---|
| 51 .......................... | 61 .......................... | 71 .......................... | 81 .......................... | 91 .......................... |
| 52 .......................... | 62 .......................... | 72 .......................... | 82 .......................... | 92 .......................... |
| 53 .......................... | 63 .......................... | 73 .......................... | 83 .......................... | 93 .......................... |
| 54 .......................... | 64 .......................... | 74 .......................... | 84 .......................... | 94 .......................... |
| 55 .......................... | 65 .......................... | 75 .......................... | 85 .......................... | 95 .......................... |
| 56 .......................... | 66 .......................... | 76 .......................... | 86 .......................... | 96 .......................... |
| 57 .......................... | 67 .......................... | 77 .......................... | 87 .......................... | 97 .......................... |
| 58 .......................... | 68 .......................... | 78 .......................... | 88 .......................... | 98 .......................... |
| 59 .......... Pay off mortgage | 69 .......................... | 79 .......................... | 89 .......................... | 99 .......................... |
| 60 ...... Retirement party | 70 ........ Party | 80 ........ Party | 90 ........ Party | 100 ...... Death |

# Benrik Address Book

**Best friends**

Very best friend...................................................................................................................................................

**Benrik Friends**

**Friends of friends**

**Casual Sex Partners**

**Loves of your life**

**Exes**

........................................................................................

........................................................................................

........................................................................................

........................................................................................

........................................................................................

........................................................................................

........................................................................................

**Enemies**

........................................................................................

........................................................................................

........................................................................................

........................................................................................

........................................................................................

........................................................................................

........................................................................................

**Vague
Acquaintances**

........................................................................................

........................................................................................

........................................................................................

........................................................................................

........................................................................................

........................................................................................

........................................................................................

**Family
(close)**

........................................................................................

........................................................................................

........................................................................................

........................................................................................

........................................................................................

........................................................................................

........................................................................................

**Family
(distant)**

........................................................................................

........................................................................................

........................................................................................

........................................................................................

........................................................................................

........................................................................................

........................................................................................

**Strangers
met whilst
drunk**

........................................................................................

........................................................................................

........................................................................................

........................................................................................

........................................................................................

........................................................................................

........................................................................................

**Other**

# Diary censorship:
# a historical overview

Over the years, the various editions of This Diary Will Change Your
Life have inevitably suffered at the hands of the censors. Here is a brief
summary of the cuts imposed and rejected. Overall they are noteworthy,
not for their sinister anti freedom-of-speech agenda, but for a sort of
awkward corporate squeamishness, and a fear of doddering old judges
making potty decisions and bankrupting everyone involved.

### This Diary Will Change Your Life 2004 (Penguin)

*Objection raised to* "Today help collapse the currency of
Bangladesh", on the grounds that Bangladeshis might not get
the joke and that Bangladesh is apparently a serious potential
market for this book. Objection overruled.

*Objection raised to* "Today, masturbate at 11.52", on the
grounds that the word "masturbate" may give offence
(suggested replacement: "pleasure yourself").
Objection overruled.

*Objection raised to* "Test if you're pregnant today" on the
grounds that asking readers to urinate on the page of a book
is in poor taste. Objection overruled.

### This Diary Will Change Your Life 2005 (Hodder)

*Objection raised to* "Speak the unspeakable today", on the
grounds that "the Virgin Mary is a slut" may constitute
blasphemy, which is still a criminal act. Objection sustained.

*Objection raised to* "Dumbing down day", on the grounds that
asking people to "snort a quick line of coke", even in the context
of arguing it makes you dumber, may constitute incitement to
take drugs. Objection imposed. Changed to "snort a quick line".

*Objection raised to* "Today help destroy an ugly building" on
grounds that "an over-enthusiastic reader might actually do it".
Change suggested to: "Kick-start a campaign for its demolition
by brushing against the building to rub off a few molecules".
Objection overruled.

*Objection raised to* "Today stalk someone". Change suggested:
"could we tone done by adding e.g. 'for 15 minutes'?"
Objection overruled.

**This Diary Will Change Your Life 2006 (Macmillan)**
*Objection raised to* "This week, cause an international security alert", on the grounds that, even though it only refers to inserting keywords like "Chechnya" in your personal emails, it could cause legal difficulties. Change to: "This week, cause an international security meltdown", which sounds more fun and light-hearted.
*Objection raised to* "Buddhist Fundamentalist Week", which advocates an armed version of the world's only peaceful religion, on the grounds that Buddhists might not get the joke. Objection overruled.
*Objection raised to* cover caption "Life is a succulent cock in the mouth of a mammoth who's hoping to spare himself from the Ice Ages by performing hideous sexual acts with whoever comes along", on the grounds that supermarkets might refuse to stock it. "Cock" changed to "phallus".

**This Diary Will Change Your Life 2007 (Macmillan)**
*Objection raised to* "This week, glorify terrorism", on the grounds that some of the examples risk giving offence. Objection overruled.
*Objection raised to* "Join extremist organizations and out-extreme them", on the grounds that it gives out the British National Party's phone number (0870 757 6267). Objection sustained. Number removed.

# Benrik Tattoos

Following popular demand, Benrik have kindly agreed to provide tattoo artwork for their fans. Simply circle the design of your choice and present it to your tattooist, or download it from www.thiswebsitewillchangeyourlife.com.

These tattoos demand advanced technical skills. Make sure your tattooist is fully qualified before proceeding.

Benrik follower: Sonja (aka Crunchtacular)
Date: 18/05/06
Tattoo parlour: Gold Coast Tattoo Parlor, 616 Lighthouse Avenue, Monterey, CA 93940 USA
Tattoo artist: "Jenny"
Comments: "The pain level was tolerable. The outlining of the tattoo was the more painful part of it all, and felt like literal cutting. Thank you Benrik."

# Benrikians of the year

These Benrik followers distinguished themselves by their service to the cause last year. May others profit by their example and follow the tasks as vigorously in 2007.

Nicka

For ending up in the Swedish tabloids

Happyjoel

For clipping his pubic hair into the shape of Richard Nixon

Pimp

For getting the Dalai Lama's position on the subject of Buddhist Fundamentalism

mr.contradiction and Hollister

For proving that opposites can indeed attract

A-Man

For winning dinner with
Benrik at the Ivy on eBay

Jade Craven

For getting a microscopic
tattoo and lying about it
pathologically

Lasr

For passing off as a
surgeon on national
radio

Riversprite

For virtual exhibitionism

Hugh

For tracking down
Jonas Jansson

Shadowy

By popular vote from
other Benrikians

Emily

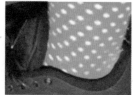

For getting fired from her
job for following Benrik

See www.thiswebsitewillchangeyourlife.com for details of their life-changing exploits and to begin recording yours…

# Benrik Limited

"Henrik"

"Ben"

You may hang these official portraits above your bed as you follow Benrik's instructions throughout 2007.

# Don't forget to register on www.thiswebsitewillchangeyourlife.com

As soon as you register, report to your Benrik Mentor. Your Benrik Mentor has been through the extreme self-improvement process before, and will help you find your feet in the early days and answer any questions or grave doubts you may have. Work out your mentor using the table below, and search for their blog on the site. Introduce yourself politely as their mentee, and take it from there! Good luck.

If your surname begins in A, your Benrik Mentor is... Happyjoel
If your surname begins in B, your Benrik Mentor is... Shadowy
If your surname begins in C, your Benrik Mentor is... Mrmonkey1980
If your surname begins in D, your Benrik Mentor is... Lucy
If your surname begins in E, your Benrik Mentor is... Wazzawazzawoo
If your surname begins in F, your Benrik Mentor is... mike.ill
If your surname begins in G, your Benrik Mentor is... Papingo
If your surname begins in H, your Benrik Mentor is... Hollisterx34
If your surname begins in I, your Benrik Mentor is... pashmina
If your surname begins in J, your Benrik Mentor is... brightpinkunicorn
If your surname begins in K, your Benrik Mentor is... slut_munkey
If your surname begins in L, your Benrik Mentor is... Nicka
If your surname begins in M, your Benrik Mentor is... Girlie
If your surname begins in N, your Benrik Mentor is... Skitzsarah
If your surname begins in O, your Benrik Mentor is... Campy
If your surname begins in P, your Benrik Mentor is... Loneranger
If your surname begins in Q, your Benrik Mentor is... BarkingBard
If your surname begins in R, your Benrik Mentor is... Camel Shoes
If your surname begins in S, your Benrik Mentor is... mikemphoto
If your surname begins in T, your Benrik Mentor is... Hugh
If your surname begins in U, your Benrik Mentor is... mr. contradiction
If your surname begins in V, your Benrik Mentor is... duckah
If your surname begins in W, your Benrik Mentor is... Nutt_E_Professor
If your surname begins in X, your Benrik Mentor is... Gabriel
If your surname begins in Y, your Benrik Mentor is... johanna
If your surname begins in Z, your Benrik Mentor is... Riversprite

Schools! Discounts available on mass orders of the Diary

Benrik would like to thank the following people, without whom the making of this Diary would not have been quite such a delight.
Extra special thanks to: Nikki Lindman and Billy Waqar for assisting Benrik. Special thanks to: Kathy Peach, Lana & Anton Delehag,
Simon Trewin, Claire Gill, Jon Butler, Linda Sima, Dusty Miller, Anna Stockbridge, Ed Ripley, Stephen Dumughn, Richard Milner,
Penny Price, Liz Johnson, Jon Mitchell, Maria Dawson, Sophie Laurimore, Andy Moreno, Emil Lanne, Ben Ruddy, Chris and Fiona,
John Hondros, Shailesh, Mark, Matthew, Guy and Marija at BGM, Trevor Franklin, Hannah Sherman and all at Monkey, Robert, Mark,
Matt, Piers, Erik, Teresa, Claudia, Brett, Catherine, Kate, Lulu, the Murderers and all at Mother, Laura Taylor, Nat Hunter, Paul Linnell,
Louise Wookey, Michael Hockney, Chris Thompson, Jens, Erik, Katie and all at Saturday, Tom, Buzz and all at Poke, Stuart and Rosco
at And, Antony Easton, Rhory Robertson, Astrid, Margaret Briffa, Silas Brown, Maija Kontto, Kate Fulton, Roman Marszalek, Marc Valli,
Aidan Onn, Sarah Aplin, Ben Riley, Addi Merrill, Rebecca Wright, Stephanie Molloy, Emanuel Edwards, Gregory Uzo, Marcia Juliana,
Richard Prue Alex & Elizabeth Carey, Aunt, Katy Follain, Antony Topping, Talulla, Stefanie Charlotte and Tommy Drews, Gaby Teresa
and Rafael Vinader, Sarah Woodruff, Emma Lowe, Daphne Fordham, Sally Evans, Alan Payne, Rebecca Bland, Clelia Uhart, Jan Lyness,
Bernard Sue & John Peach, Kenneth & Anna-Lena & Lovisa & Hjalmar & Elin Delehag, Fredrik Nordbeck, Eva Edsjö.

www.thiswebsitewillchangeyourlife.com

All illustrations, photography, design and typography by Benrik, except as follows. Where the work is not property and copyright of the
authors, all attempts have been made by the authors to contact correct copyright holders. The authors would like to gratefully thank for
permission to include the following within this edition: Official author portraits © Lana Ivanyukhina. Week 9 photos © Christian Coinbergh.
Week 25 photo © Jon Bergman. Week 33 and 35 illustrations © Lana Ivanyukhina. Tattoo photo © Crunchtacular. Benrikians photos
© themselves. Week 40 E. Klawitter/ zefa / Corbis. Getty Images: Week 13 © Stuart McClymont; Week 20 © George Doyle; Week 32
© John Lund; Week 37 newspaper © Digital Vision, tables © Dana Edmunds, radio © Michael Wildsmith, hats © Gary John Norman,
TV © Michael Dunning, pickup truck © Susan Barr, sleep © David Oliver, beach © Peter Denton; Week 38 © Image Source; Week 43 earth
core © Jason Reed, road up © Hulton Archive, hole in ground © Hulton Archive; Week 45 © Robert Cameron; Week 49 © Peter Dazeley;
Week 50 © Peter Dazeley; Week 51 © Frank Oberle; Week 52 © Chad Baker. "When the Lilliputians…" © James Gleick in Faster,
The Acceleration of Just About Everything, (Abacus 1999). Thank you to all the Benrik readers who sent in ideas once again this year,
and in particular to those whose ideas were selected: Week 5 © Simon "Wazzawazzawoo" Voysey; Week 7 © Linda "Fiu" Lönnqvist; Week
10 © Joel Moss Levinson and Sami; Week 15 © Alex Marshall; Week 20 © Katherine "incompletia" Calvert; Week 25 © Jay Glover; Week
33 © Kelsey Grist; Week 34 © Lorilei Storm; Week 37 (part of) © Matt Welland; Week 43 © Erin Napier and Rover; Week 45 © Adam
"peculiar23" Dolsen. If there is further enquiry, please contact the authors c/o PFD, Drury House, 34-43 Russell St, London WC2B 5HA, UK.

First published 2006 by Boxtree
An imprint of Pan Macmillan Ltd
Pan Macmillan, 20 New Wharf Road, London N1 9RR
Basingstoke and Oxford
Associated companies throughout the world
www.panmacmillan.com

ISBN-13: 978-0752-22617-0
ISBN-10: 0-7522-2617-7

9 8 7 6 5 4 3 2 1

A CIP catalogue record for this book is available from the British Library.
Colour reproduction by Aylesbury Studios Bromley Ltd.
Printed and bound in Great Britain by Butler & Tanner.

Your Values Are Our Toilet Paper